Documents of Interaction

University of Florida Monographs

Social Sciences No. 74

Documents of Interaction:
Biography, Autobiography, and Life History in Social Science Perspective

Michael V. Angrosino

University of Florida Press
Gainesville

Library of Congress Cataloging-in-Publication Data

Angrosino, Michael V.
  Documents of interaction.

  (University of Florida monographs. Social sciences ; no. 74)
  Bibliography: p.
  Includes index.
  1. Social sciences—Biographical methods. I. Title.
II. Series
H61.29.A54   1989   300'.722   88-26129
ISBN 0-8130-0925-1 (alk. paper)

University Presses of Florida is the central agency for scholarly publishing of the State of Florida's university system, producing books selected for publication by the faculty editorial committees of Florida's nine public universities: Florida A&M University Press (Tallahassee), Florida Atlantic University Press (Boca Raton), Florida International University Press (Miami), Florida State University Press (Tallahassee), University of Central Florida Press (Orlando), University of Florida Press (Gainesville), University of North Florida Press (Jacksonville), University of South Florida Press (Tampa), University of West Florida Press (Pensacola).

  Orders for books published by all member presses should be addressed to University Presses of Florida, 15 NW 15th Street, Gainesville, FL 32603.

Contents

Preface

> However creatively one travels, however deep an experience in childhood or middle age, it takes thought (a sifting of impulses, ideas, and references that become more multifarious as one grows older) to understand what one has lived through or where one has been.
>
> —V. S. Naipaul, *Finding the Center*

WHEN THIS BOOK was in its first draft, I wrote to Freddie, the protagonist of chapter 3. He has known and worked with me for the better part of two decades, and he is used to seeing himself discussed in some of my academic writings. This time I sent him the entire book because I was curious to see how he would respond to research conducted with other people, for different purposes. He wrote back: "As usual, you have caught me to a T. Hey Mikey—isn't it time you started calling me by my rightful name? If anybody ever reads your stuff they must know me so well by now they could as well know my real name. But that other business? Is just blague [gossip] you know. Nobody going to care about none of that."

I have respectfully ignored Freddie's advice and have left him cloaked in his accustomed pseudonym, but the rest of his commentary was harder to shake off. On one level, he was speaking as one who usually stands alone in the spotlight of my scholarly scrutiny, a situation he very much enjoys even when my analysis of his behavior is less than flattering. He clearly did not care to be simply part of the crowd in this new book. But, on a deeper level, he was asking the very question that had impelled me to compose this study in the first place: Why should we continue to be interested in the old but so frequently maligned "life history" approaches to social research? Haven't those approaches left us with a huge literature of highly paraticularistic, often decontextualized accounts of questionable relevance to the study of the larger processes of culture, history, or personality? In the last analysis, didn't they really amount to *blague*—interesting but essentially irrelevant gossip?

Since I have so often turned to some of the life history approach in my research, I devoutly hoped that the techniques associated with that approach had some larger value. So I set out to contribute to the growing social scientific discourse on the potentialities and limitations of personalistic, humanistic, interpretive studies of social/cultural/historical phenomena. I have done so by using my own research for illustration, but not because I think of it as paradigmatic of any one style of life history research. Rather, I present my own material because I am most familiar with it.

It is also true that I have come to realize that the things I most want to understand about the ways in which individuals relate to their society, culture, and historical moment have not entirely yielded to the methods I have been using all along. So the book ends with a description of my ongoing project in which an alternative method for dealing with autobiography is used. This method seeks generalizable truths about individuals and their culture not in the paraticular content of their lives but in the symbolic cues they marshal in the effort to share their lives with significant others.

This book reflects a debt to my teachers and friends Julia Crane, who engendered in me a career-long fascination with the study of lives in process, and James Peacock, who opened up to me the endlessly tempting cafeteria of ideas that is "symbolic anthropology." This study also shows the influence of the late Nicholas Hobbs, who never ceased to remind his students and colleagues that even in the midst of "scholarly apparatus" *people* still count.

The research projects described herein were supported by the Foreign Area Fellowship Program, the National Endowment for the Humanities, and the National Institute of Mental Health. I want to thank Harry Collymore, Chris Nath, Nan Martin, and

Edward Whyte for having facilitated and nurtured aspects of my research. This manuscript has benefited greatly from the comments of L. L. Langness and two anonymous reviewers for the University of Florida Press.

I acknowledge the clerical assistance of Virginia Williams and the good offices of the Suncoast Mental Health Associates for the production of the manuscript. A special thanks is owed to my own students who have so patiently suffered through the process of developing my thinking on this subject.

I recently wrote back to Freddie in the wake of submitting a final draft of the manuscript to the publisher: "I hope it has come out as more than *blague*. I hope that while the research I talk about shares some of the same raw material with common gossip, it has the potential for helping us catch a glimpse of the common human experience, even in the face of all the little details that make us different. If it does that, you will be at least partly responsible, because you helped me understand that a life, even of a person sometimes scorned by society, *is* important, if only we know where and how to look for its meaning."

1 /
Life Histories in Social Research: Issues and Definitions

IN HISTORICAL, sociological, psychological, and anthropological research, biographical and autobiographical materials have long been considered important resources. In the humanities, too, these genres have been diligently studied, not only because of their artistic merits but also for the insights they may provide into the process of creative thought or the cultural ambience of artistic production.

This monograph is primarily concerned with life accounts that are basically autobiographical. It does not review the entire range of applications of life history methods in the social and behavioral sciences and the humanities. Its purpose is to suggest that autobiographical materials are most fruitfully treated as documents of interaction between a subject recounting his or her life experiences and an audience, either the researcher recording the story or the readers of the resulting text. The audience, I contend, plays a vital, creative role in the formation of the story; it is not a passive recipient of information. This view of the role of the audience augments the more conventional view of autobiographical texts as documents of the author's consciousness only.

The use and interpretation of autobiographical materials in social research appears to be in crisis. Biographies and autobiographies may, of course, have intrinsic literary value, but the data found in them have generally been held to be useful primarily to the extent that they conform to three key assumptions: (1) a story told at a particular historical moment is representative of patterns forming the personality of individuals and the character of their culture; (2) individuals (or selected groups of them) typify their entire culture; and (3) the researcher is simply a neutral recorder of factual data.

1

These assumptions have a certain surface validity. Written biographical materials of well-known individuals can be verified against the established facts of a given historical period as determined from other sources. Life histories collected by anthropologists and oral historians can similarly be verified against more general ethnographic accounts of their community of origin. It has seemed reasonable to conclude, therefore, that social scientists have had the means to confirm the factual basis of the life accounts of individuals and that they could disregard any accounts they could not verify.

Because all analysis in anthropology, sociology, psychology, and history rests on the ability to discern patterns in events and behaviors, a common tendency is to emphasize the normative in reconstructing an exotic community or a bygone era. If a culture can thus be analyzed in terms of its central tendencies, and if individual life stories are subject to rigorous verification, then the individual life can be used to represent some of the general tendencies of the culture and era.

It is this position that has come increasingly under critical scrutiny during the past decade, despite its superficial logicality and the impressive and influential body of sociohistorical knowledge it has generated. To what extent does this syllogism need to be modified? If it is modified, to what extent is the methodology of the life history as a whole called into question?

These issues inform the discussion that follows. Suggested responses to these questions will be approached first by examining what current literary theory tells about the genres of biography and autobiography. It may then be possible to apply some of these insights in a social science context. This review will include comparative critical analyses of three of the author's own life history–oriented research projects illustrating three traditional ways in which such data can be used in social research. Finally, a fourth project will be analyzed to present an alternative way to integrate the autobiographical genre into the theory and method of social research.

A note on terminology is in order. This essay adopts the usage most consistent with the study of literary genres (see, for example, Spengemann 1980). *Biography* will refer to the narrative account of one person's life as written or otherwise recorded by another, reconstructed mainly, though not exclusively, from records and archives.* *Autobiography* will pertain to the narrative account of a person's life that he or she has personally written or otherwise recorded. *Life history* will refer to the account of one person's life "as told to" another, the researcher.† The term *life story* will be used to distinguish narratives (which may belong to the biographical, autobiographical, or life history categories) that purport to record the entire span of a life from those that tend to highlight a few key events or focus on a few significant relationships or dwell on perceived "turning points." These last three types of accounts, which can belong to any of the three broader categories, will be termed *personal narratives*.

By convention, *biography* has been used as a convenient rubric to cover all such materials (see, for example, Bertaux 1981b). This usage reflects the priority that literary criticism has placed on the act of retelling or interpreting a person's life; it emphasizes the separate textual reality of the resulting biographical document. In essence, someone's life is only raw data until they are given analytical shape by the biographer. Current literary theory recognizes autobiography as a separate genre, or at least as a subgenre because of the special epistemological and

---

* Literary theory permits the term *biography* as well as other terms discussed in this paragraph to be applied to nonnarrative forms such as poetry or drama. It also extends the terms to "fictionalized" life accounts (see, for example, Eakin 1985). Such genre are rarely used in social science contexts, though the author does not wish to exclude the possibility of their incorporation into social research. The word *narrative* will be used throughout to specify a form of writing, but it should not be interpreted as referring solely to prose nonfiction accounts.

† Mandelbaum (1973:177), in an influential article, has restricted the term *life history* to accounts that emphasize the experiences and requirements of individuals and how they cope with society. He uses the term *life cycle studies* for accounts that, by contrast, emphasize the process of socialization and enculturation, processes by which the society molds the individual. Also influential in some circles in Bertaux's (1981b:7) distinction between the *life story,* an oral account of a person's own life, and the *life history,* a life story augmented with biographical and other data from other sources. In this essay, the term *life history* is used in the more general sense already described.

psychological issues related to the recounting of one's own life, whether spontaneously or as elicited by a researcher. If biography, as the term is conventionally used, focuses on the finished product, autobiography focuses on the act of telling. But, like biography, it gives priority to the process of analysis except that the interpreter and the subject in this case are the same person. This essay will develop an alternative point of view.

Traditional studies of autobiography have stressed the dichotomy between the teller (one-who-lives-the-life) and the hearer (one-who-interprets-the-life). Even in autobiography, the interpreter must maintain a critical, objective distance from his or her own life in order to create a "factual" account of it. Contrarily, this essay focuses on the relationship between the teller and the hearer; the critical "text" will not be the end-product narrative version of the life but the "drama" of interaction, the process that generates the narrative. The title of this study deliberately eschews the more familiar generic labels and refers to all biographical and autobiographical materials as "documents of interaction," specifically the interaction between the individual reliving and reinterpreting life experiences and the individual whose *active* responses to that telling become an integral part of its process of creation. This essay is not an argument for the abandonment of traditional analytical concepts associated with biographical materials in the social sciences or with the interpretation of autobiography as a literary genre. Rather, this work suggests another way of developing the method and interpreting the results.

2 /
The Genre of Autobiography: A Conceptual Background

THE STUDY OF documents of interaction begins with a consideration of the emergence of autobiography as a literary genre distinct from biography. Because literary critics have, over the past two decades, drawn increasingly sharp distinctions between the two types, the issues of concern as these materials are applied to social research have emerged with greater clarity.

Autobiography as Literature

Literary criticism was slow to deal specifically with autobiography because, though it often took a familiar literary form, it frequently dealt with personal materials in a direct way that was not always readily recognizable as "art." Moreover, the autobiography is, by definition, "incomplete" since "the end of the story" can never be written. Most importantly, the autobiography is self-reflexive; it appropriates the critical function to itself, and therefore sometimes leaves critics to deal not with a text (the task for which they are trained) but with the writer's own view of that text, a psychological rather than a literary function (Olney 1980: 24–25). An autobiography used to be taken quite literally as a "factual account of the writer's life" (Spengemann 1980:xi). It was, indeed, viewed merely as a "self-written biography." That being the case, it was expected to employ biographical means and to be subject to the same standards of historical verification (Spengemann 1980:xii).

However, autobiography, which has been described as being simultaneously the "least complicated of writing performances" and "the most elusive of literary documents" (Olney 1980:3), proved to be too difficult to pin down in that way. For one thing, much material that is revelatory about major figures (particularly

5

those in the arts) has been produced in the guise of fiction or of philosophical discourse. These documents may have skimped on specific biographical detail, but they have been crucial to understanding the mind of influential persons. Critical opinion was loath to set all these data aside just because they were not strictly "historical," and so a perception of a separate genre, with slightly more flexible canons of analysis, was born. Spengemann (1980:170–245) has comprehensively reviewed the landmarks in the evolution of autobiography and in formulating a critical approach to the genre (see also Bruss 1976).

One aspect of this history that is of particular concern to the social scientist is the way in which autobiography has become the "focalizing literature for various 'studies' (e.g., American studies, Afro-American studies, women's studies) that otherwise have little by way of a defining, organizing center to them" (Olney 1980:13). Because autobiography is the "story of a distinctive culture written in individual characters and from within," it has been used to offer a "privileged access to an experience . . . that no other variety of writing can offer" (Olney 1980:13).

This feature has been especially important in the growth of Afro-American studies since so much of the early black experience in the New World was preserved in autobiographical reminiscences rather than in more formal historical archives and since so many prominent black writers (Frederick Douglass, Malcolm X, Olaudah Equiano, Maya Angelou, among many others) entered the literary mainstream via the autobiography (Olney 1980:15; see also Blasing 1977, Blassingame 1973).

In this monograph, autobiographies will be treated as emanations of individuals and as reflections of their will to reveal and share part of their selves. That essential act of sharing, of course, presupposes listeners/readers whose anticipated response makes them active participants in the creation of the autobiography.

The autobiographical narrative does not simply recount a life; it can logically only reflect facets of that life—some of them unintentional but most of them deliberately chosen. The selection process is a reflection of the "world view" of the autobiographer (Olney 1972:4), the image of the surroundings that he or she holds and wishes to convey to others. The autobiography, therefore, cannot be straight reportage about one's life and times. It is a highly selective view of that life and its sociohistorical context, a view that mirrors the author's philosophical predispositions, political biases, or simply the grinding of personal axes. These slants are "revelatory," of course, but extreme caution is required lest we assume the author's world view uncritically as if it were the historical truth.

Much the same thing could be said about biography. Even the most revered classic of that genre, Boswell's *Life of Johnson,* can scarcely be said to be without personal bias. But Boswell is usually pardoned because he was a "character" in his own right. Scholarly writers of modern biography, on the other hand, are expected to be much more objective in their chronicles. Creators of autobiography, by contrast, are allowed some leeway in reconstructing history from their own points of view.

A variant of this position has been expressed by Jean-Paul Sartre, who contends that, since all memory is selective, there must be a "prior structure of personal identity that provides the template by which certain events are cast as images significant enough to be stored" (Langness and Frank 1981:109). In his study of Jean Genet (1963), Sartre suggests that this template takes the form of the subject's "fundamental project," which is "the organizing principle or nexus of meanings and values that inform a person's choices" (in Langness and Frank 1981:109). This fundamental project, which may be the result of a social labeling process, gives the individual something to live for. No matter how scattered people's lives may appear, all of their choices will be governed by the fundamental project. The problem with this view, however, is that, when only an autobiographical text is available as a guide, it is impossible to know if real choices are involved or simply retrospective rationalizations of choices already made (Crapanzano 1984:959; see also Earle 1972, Mehlman 1974).

From the standpoint of the literary critic, it is possible to assert that each individual is unique and that it is therefore unlikely that anyone would take the trouble to write or record an autobiography just to prove that he or she was simply one of the crowd. An autobiography is therefore a record of individuality, and often the bias that stands behind the production of the text is one that exaggerates the individuality even further.

Autobiographies, then, illuminate diversity, not generality. Ferrarotti (1981:20), for example, stresses the specificity of data derived from biographical materials. These materials are essentially the elements of idiographic analysis, he contends, and do not lend themselves to nomothetic processes. Yet at least two generations of social scientists have used autobiographical data as if they were, in fact, illustrations of general patterns of culture.

Bertaux (1981a:44), for one, is not troubled by this problem, feeling that sociological researchers should abandon their pretense to scientific positivism. He outlines a program for a "humanistic" sociology by suggesting that life history materials renew a sense of appreciation for the art of narrative, which is valuable in and of itself. When social researchers describe a culture or a society or a community or an era, they are, in fact, telling a story about it, and so they have much to learn about the proper techniques of story telling.

On the other hand, even for a practicing literary critic or humanistic social scientist, there must be natural limits to the view that each life is unique and hence each autobiography is also unique. After all, literary criticism, no less than social research, is predicated on the ability to discern general patterns, the better to facilitate comparative judgments.

But I suggest that the source of usable generalizations is the form that the creators of autobiography select to convey their evocation of self. Even an individual as bizarre as Hitler, whose specific psychological demons were not, one assumes, universally shared, could still write an autobiography that sold well and moved many people even before he came to power. He did it by presenting his private, warped preoccupations in the guise of pastoral childhood scenes, in images of family conflict common to German culture, and through celebrations of the redemptive force of youthful camaraderie that reverberated against a millennium of German history.

In sum, Hitler clothed himself in literary forms and cultural resonances that were appealing to his audience, even to those of its members to whom the naked message of his political philosophy might have been distasteful. Hitler was such a genius at manipulating form over content that *Mein Kampf* stands not simply as the record of a unique madman but also as a recognizable example of literary process (see Erikson 1963: 326–58). The same devices he used to evoke the darkness of his image of self and his world view could have been used by any German of the period wishing to celebrate the positive side of life. Autobiographers create, in effect, metaphors of their selves by means of common literary devices.

The fact that personal experiences can be consciously shaped by means of stylistic devices that link our private worlds to the experiences of others indicates that, even if the content of our "selves" is unique, the form through which we convey our self-perceptions and world views is capable of being shared. The formal properties of this act of sharing—which makes the autobiography a fundamentally social fact—may be studied in a critical, comparative manner, even if the unique, specific, personal content of the self remains forever unknowable—perhaps even to the autobiographer. An anthropologist might point out that autobiography uses forms evocative of shared experiences by which individuals are socialized. The autobiography taps the common, unspoken processes of the ritualized norms of behavior typical of a particular culture.

In any case, it might be suggested at this point that, whatever the source of that formal commonality, verifiable truth in the autobiography rests not in the historical facts of the life account but in the degree to which the autobiographer's chosen metaphors of self communicate to and link up with his or her intended audience. As Starobinski (1980:77) has suggested, the production of autobiography requires not only a sense that personal experience is intrinsically valuable, but a belief that the recounting of that experience offers "an opportunity for a sincere relation with someone else."

Thus autobiography is by definition a product of the creative imagination, even if it takes the form of a straightforward, historical prose narrative. Renza (1980:269) makes the point even more explicitly when he states that autobiography "transforms empirical facts into artifacts." He adds that not only can autobiography possibly encompass works of fiction but that it is, by definition, fiction. But, of course, "fictional" by no means implies "untrue." As Mandel (1980:49) puts it, "Strictly speaking, autobiography is not a recollection of one's life. Of course, everyone has recollections and memories. Memories are common phenomena—familiar, comfortable, inevitable. They are also spontaneous and natural. An autobiography, on the other hand, is an artifact, a construct wrought from words."

Hankiss (1981) has likened the process of writing an autobiography to an act of "mythological rearranging" and has provided a useful typology of basic strategies by which this rearrangement can be accomplished:

1. If the present self-image of writers is good and they wish to assert that this present positive state flows from good childhood or other early experiences, then they adopt a dynastic strategy in casting the events of life into the "mythological" framework of an autobiography. In such an autobiography, childhood is mythically embellished as a source of strength. The writer's parents, or other significant adult role models, are upheld as the fountainheads of enduring values. It is also from these strong adults that the writer learns the attitude "We are different from other people." This difference may or may not be a factor of inherited wealth or social prominence. But even people who come from a modest socioeconomic background will interpret their parentally derived values as a call to some sort of honorable service to society, of the performance of good works, or of the exercise of political leadership.

2. If the present self-image of writers is good but they see childhood and early life negatively, then an antithetical strategy will be adopted. The writers tend to see their present strengths as virtues resulting from self-will and determination to overcome

the limitations of early life, or from a deliberate revolt against unacceptable parental standards. The antithetical autobiographer tends to have a highly developed sense of being a "self-made" individual, without true antecedents.

3. If the present self-image of writers is bad but they look back to childhood as a positive time, they will adopt a compensatory strategy. The autobiographer harks back to the values learned in childhood as if to say, "I may be rotten now, but I have a good background." Such autobiographies are chronicles of falls from grace. Implicit in this strategy is the feeling that, if only the writer can get back in touch with those old-time virtues, then perhaps he or she can rise out of the muck. The production of the autobiography itself may be part of that process of rediscovery.

4. If the present self-image of writers is bad and they regard their childhood as the source of that negativity, a self-absolutory strategy will be adopted, as if to say, "How could I have turned out good—look where I came from!"

Hankiss's overall point is that the thematic structure of an autobiography is not accidental. It is essential that the writer make a personal assessment and try to figure out why he or she is like that. Everything else flows from this fundamental act of insight, which is then transformed by fictional means into a story that will communicate that discovered odyssey of self to others. The autobiographer has reason to assume that the four strategies will strike responsive chords with the intended audience and will select a thematic structure that will not only satisfy internal needs but will also convey a desirable image to the audience.

For example, mainstream U.S. values lead to a preference for Horatio Alger types, who, by pluck and initiative, rise above their circumstances. We are a bit put off by what can come off as the smugness of those who "carry on the tradition," are scornful of those who "blow" early advantages, and are usually downright hostile to those who appear to wallow in adversity and then whine about how they never had any breaks. The classic middle-American autobiography, such as that of Ben Franklin, is thus antithetical in style, and our popular mythology tends to treat examples of this type as "inspirational."

By contrast, some of the most powerful black autobiographies, such as those of Malcolm X or Eldridge Cleaver (in his *Soul on Ice* days) adopt an accusatory, self-absolutory strategy. Such stories strike a responsive note in black readers but are often uncomfortably threatening to white middle-class readers. For politicized blacks in the 1960s, these may have been precisely the responses desired from polarized communities. It is difficult to imagine the Cleaver of the 1960s wanting to write a rags-to-riches story that would have edified a white audience, even if that were somehow the way he saw himself then. In adopting the self-absolutory tone, he was offering a critique of mainstream U.S. society, which was responsible for the institutionalized racism that he saw as the source of his problems and against which he was compelled to react.

To summarize, the movement among literary critics to treat autobiography as a separate genre has raised the following issues:

1. The "life" account document may take many forms, including, but certainly not limited to, the straightforward historical records.

2. This document need not be subject to traditional standards of historical verification.

3. The truth of a document recording someone's "life" is gauged by its capacity to connect with the experiences of its intended audience, not by its conformity with established "fact."

4. The "self" behind the "life story" is less important than the self that is created in the process of communication between a writer and an audience.

5. The literary devices that communicate this "metaphor of self" are derived from, sanctioned by, and given meaning through the culture that the writer and the audience share.

I will now turn to applications of the life history method in social research to see how these literary insights may enrich the social science perspective.

Personal Documents as Resources for
Social Research: Traditional Views

Biographical materials were enthusiastically included among the resources that could be tapped by the emerging scientific disciplines of history, sociology, and anthropology in the nineteenth century. Such materials were always most closely associated with advocates of those theoretical approaches that emphasized the importance of subjectivity in social processes (Kohli 1981:63).

For example, the pioneering sociohistorians Thomas and Znaniecki produced a massive and influential study of the Polish peasantry and the migration of many peasants to America (originally published 1917–18). They made extensive use of what they called "life records," which they pronounced "the perfect type of sociological material" (in Barnouw 1985:248). "Life stories" were a major focus of the influential Chicago School of sociology in the 1920s and 1930s (Bertaux 1981b:5), and they remained an integral feature of sociological research until the 1950s, when the demand for quantitative rigor limited their utility (Bertaux 1981b:1; see also Angell 1945). Although Franz Boas, the "father" of American anthropology, dismissed life histories as "essays in retrospective falsification" (in Barnouw 1985:248), his students made extensive use of them, and orally recorded life histories have never really fallen from favor among anthropologists. (See, for example, the classic statement by Kluckhohn 1945, as well as more recent reviews by Langness 1965 and Langness and Frank 1981.)

And, to be sure, a modern approach to history would be inconceivable without the collaboration of those who record or interpret biographical data. Furthermore, attempts to standardize a methodology for the collection and interpretation of such materials by social researchers of various disciplinary traditions have a long and distinguished pedigree (Dollard 1935).

There are two major approaches to the use of these data. North American scholars have tended to favor the study of the individual life story as a sociohistorical document, complete and revealing in its own right, and their European counterparts have generally focused on collective accounts. In typical American scholarship, the "extraordinary" individual has often been seen as the representative of the otherwise anonymous many. This outlook has no doubt been encouraged by the experience of U.S. anthropologists, who are influential pioneers in the use of life history in social research because they were often in the position of reconstructing entire vanished tribal cultures from the reminiscences of elderly survivors. Typical European research, by contrast, used the recorded reminiscences collected widely from among those "faceless" masses in order to construct an image of (presumably intact) society as a whole.

The most outstanding example of this European approach —albeit one unfortunately known to us only through very fragmentary translations—is that of the Polish scholar Josef Chalasiński, a student of Znaniecki. Beginning shortly after World War I, Chalasiński and his students organized literally hundreds of public competitions in which local cultural agencies awarded prizes for the best essays of personal memoirs. This effort was shelved during World War II but was resumed shortly thereafter and continued into the 1950s. The process resulted in the collection of thousands of *pamietniki,* written autobiographies (Bertaux 1981b:2).

Chalasiński's impulse was not strictly sociological; an ardent nationalist living in an era of national reunification, he must have felt it politically vital to keep his compatriots in touch with their cultural traditions and to help them identify with their fellow Poles after centuries of partition and foreign domination. The process of using scholarship for the political purpose of reviving a sense of national unity was repeated (less comprehensively, to be sure) elsewhere in Europe, and differs sharply from the American effort to pin the single elusive specimen for microscopic study.

The use of autobiography in the American style was probably shaped by the strong influence of psychology on the social sciences in general in the United States. Even in the heyday of the Chicago School, which supposedly emphasized the social group and its "ecology," sociologists working in that tradition began to incorporate the techniques of psychological analysis into their studies of group phenomena. (See, for example, Allport 1945; Babad, Birnbaum, and Benne 1983.)

Clifford Shaw, for one, studied the phenomenon of juvenile delinquency in the 1920s; his technique was to ask boys on parole to write their "own stories," to which he added whatever other relevant material he could glean from police and court records as well as from medical and psychiatric findings. Following medicopsychiatric usage, he called the results "case histories" (Shaw 1930). Although he believed that they could be used to formulate generalizations about the social problems at hand, in fact they were (and remain) interesting primarily as documentary glimpses into particular lives. Then, as now, the bias in Shaw's sampling technique prevented his case histories from being used seriously as the bases of analytical generalizations, although some present-day sociologists, more careful about sampling, continue to advocate the use of selected "case studies" as means to "generalize to the larger organizational nexus" (Denzin 1981:149). One other criticism of the case study approach has been that it tends to focus on deviants. A noteworthy exception is the work of White (1952), who selected a group of "normal" subjects (as determined by a battery of psychological tests) and followed them longitudinally through their autobiographical writings.

In reflecting on the two major styles of personal documentation research, Bertaux (1981a:39) notes that the life stories of significant individuals can often stand on their own; even if we reject the contention that these peoples' lives "represent" a larger society, we can still be drawn in by the psychological resonances they set up with us, as individuals. Collective life histories, by contrast, are more problematic. Except for those like the Chalasiński *pamietniki,* which were collected for a purpose that explicitly transcended a research function, collections of life histories do not readily speak for themselves. It may be said that such collections form an impressionistic mosaic of the society, but in fact they cannot do even that if they are left as raw data. Bertaux's conclusion is that, whatever the purely literary value of an unadorned autobiography may be, it is useless to the social researcher without the full, mediating cooperation of the researcher (1981a:44).

This position echoes that of Thomas and Znaniecki, who postulated that every social fact was the product of a "continual interaction of individual consciousness and objective social reality" (1958:1831). The production of an autobiography is itself part of the process of the evolution of individual consciousness (Schutz and Luckmann 1974), and the construction of a life history "is the mode by which the individual represents those aspects of his past which are relevant to the present situation" (Kohli 1981:65). Life histories can, of course, never be collections of all the events of a person's life; they are thus "structured self-images" reflective of the "identity" the subject chooses to present.

But, though autobiographical "self-thematization" is part of an "internal cognitive process" (Kohli 1981:65), it has no social meaning unless a significant other receives the message and feeds back a response. The researcher, who arranges and interprets those data and, in many cases, elicits them in the first place, is thus a critical midwife in the birthing of a social (as opposed to an internalized) sense of self.

It is thus the researcher's duty to supply the theme that links the experiences of individual informants into a collective whole, just as he or she must clarify the assumptions that stand behind the assertion that the life of an individual somehow typifies the whole. Perhaps the most commonly selected theme in life history–oriented research has been that of social change, which has figured prominently in research in sociology, anthropology, and history (Elder 1981:78; see also Balan, Browning, and Jelin 1973). It is possible to document the details of this change, but a sense of its impact and how it is dealt with comes through best via the lives of people caught up in the process. Socialization (how people learn to be members of their community) and aging (how they pass through the crises of the life cycle as defined by their culture) have also been popular themes linking collective life histories (Elder 1981:78).

Alternative Views

Some theoreticians would go beyond the thematization function in analyzing the role of the researcher in the life history process. As Catani (1981:212) has stated so simply, "The work [the life history] is above all the product of an encounter." The textual product of that encounter may well contain vital documentary data. But, unless the encounter that generates such data is kept in mind, that text is apt to be misinterpreted. The exchange between subject and researcher is "symbolic" in that it is ritualized via patterns of speech and other forms of communication (body language, gesture, details of hospitality). It could not be otherwise, because the exchange involves "that which our civilization deems to be the most precious of goods; that is, oneself" (Catani 1981:212).

This ritualized encounter may be observed when the life stories under consideration are produced in one setting and then interpreted by researchers in another (as in Chalasiński's work), or when the biographies of deceased historical personages are being scrutinized. But the encounter is most obvious in classic anthropological and oral historical research when the subject and researcher are in face-to-face contact, and where the production of the life history is a joint effort, although the technology of the tape recorder provides the illusion of first-person autobiography even in these cases (Bertaux 1981b:8; Catani 1975). There are some notable "collective" life histories in the anthropological and oral historical literature (Oscar Lewis's "family autobiographies" are perhaps the best known), but even they tend to have been collected "one-on-one" and assembled by later editorial process.

Some anthropologists have championed a "personalistic" approach to ethnography in general (e.g., Spiro 1972) that would focus on the impact of the individual on culture, rather than vice versa; the research process termed *life history* by Mandelbaum would fit this style. Although anthropologists and oral historians are often eager to personalize the field in another sense, by speaking anecdotally about "my people" or "my village," they have traditionally been reluctant to treat their role in the research process as if it were a relevant ethnographic fact.

Training manuals speak extensively of the need to establish rapport, and they detail the conventional techniques for conducting effective interviews, but there is a tacit assumption that, once those fundamentals have been taken care of, what unfolds is the pure outpouring of the respondent's consciousness. The ways in which the researcher manipulates the encounter, or the ways in which the informant deals with that manipulation and tries to manipulate the situation in turn, have rarely been discussed. Critical discussions of life history methodology center on questions of sampling, methods of recording data, and styles of presentation (Barnouw 1985:249)—all in an effort to establish the objective veracity of the resulting text.

Most practitioners of the life history method would agree with Barnouw's assessment that "some of the best life history documents are those which show the least prodding on the part of the ethnographer" (1985:251). They would probably also second his complaint that published life history texts rarely make it clear whether the data were spontaneous or were elicited by "digging"—the implication being that the prudent reader could then disregard the latter.

Many anthropologists and oral historians feel that editing spoils the natural flow of a subject's inner consciousness. The famous autobiography of Sun Chief (Simmons 1942) was criticized by Kluckhohn (1945:97) for having been edited into a piece of literature, as much the product of the ethnographer's consciousness as it was of the Indian's. On the other hand, the extensive psychologically oriented life story collection by Cora Du Bois on Alor (1944) may be said to suffer from a lack of editing (Barnouw 1985: 252) since we never quite know what all the accounts add up to. It can be assumed that at least some of Du Bois's informants falsified their accounts (either deliberately—to tease the foreigner—or inadvertently—because they misunderstood what she was getting at). Because orthodox Freudian theory suggests that even "false" data can be psychologically revealing if a pattern can be discerned in them, it would presumably have been helpful had the researcher been more forthcoming in her indication of what was "false" and what was "true." In either case, the criticism reflects a concern with the accuracy of the text as either ethnographic, historical, or psychological data.

Some researchers (Gladwin and Sarason 1953; Henry 1945), in fact, have taken the position that since such textual accuracy can never be satisfactorily established—particularly when dealing with subjects from cultures in which the generation of autobiographical data is not highly valued—then such documents should not even be suggested as having analytical psychocultural value. Similarly, much of the criticism of Lewis's popular œuvre (Lewis 1961, 1968; Lewis, Lewis, and Rigdon 1977) rests on the perception that he edited and organized his material extensively to bring out certain ideological themes but presented the texts as if they were "raw data." His method has been unfavorably compared with that of Catani (1973), who actually published the raw interviews as appendices to the finished life histories (Bertaux 1981b:8).

The most cogent dissent from this mainstream view is currently being voiced by the anthropologist Vincent Crapanzano, whose own study, *Tuhami: Portrait of a Moroccan* (1980), was among the first to treat explicitly the ethnographer's role in shaping the final text. His discussion of his relationship with his informant (and with an interpreter who also worked on the project) is presented without apology and without any intent to clear away the resulting "falsification" so as to establish a "pure" text. The text is treated as inevitably the product of a particular interaction among specific people in a defined context. Wilson's engaging and moving *Oscar* (1974) is less widely known, and Wilson himself has not made his analytical point of view as much an issue as has Crapanzano, but it is an important work reflecting the same general tendency.

Crapanzano has gone on to offer a more general critique of the conventional life history approach. He contends (1984:954) that personal documents have all too often been used by social scientists trying to leaven the impersonality of ethnographic and historical reportage with something that speaks of the intensely personal experiences of fieldwork. As a result, a lack of true analysis is often attached to these documents; instead there is "commentary," which "can be saccharine in its sentimentality and overambitious in its justification" (1984:954). He offers a significant distinction between the use of personalistic interview techniques to elicit specific data—an acceptable function of ethnographic and historical "science"—and the use of the "life history" itself as if it were a body of data.

There are, according to Langness and Frank (1981:24), six reasons for the use of biographical materials in social research: to portray a culture; for literary purposes; to portray aspects of culture change; to illustrate an aspect of culture not usually portrayed by other means (for example, women's views); to communicate something not otherwise communicated (for example, the "insider's" view of a culture); and to say something about deviance.

Except possibly for the second of these traditional functions, all of them seem to require at least a provisional establishment of the textual authenticity of the life history. But, Crapanzano asks, how do you "confirm" a life history account—how do you provide an independent witness for a life? Certainly careful fieldworkers in intimate contact with their informants would be able to spot some inconsistencies, but "it would seem that consistency of accounts over time and among informants is rather more revealing of a cultural orientation or psychological disposition than of the actual occurrence of an event" (1984:955). Crapanzano therefore suggests that

> The life history . . . is the result of a complex self-constituting negotiation. It is the product (at least from the subject's point of view) of an arbitrary and peculiar demand from another—the anthropologist. (At some level the anthropologist's demand is always a response to the informant.) The interplay . . . of demand and desire governs much of the content of the life history, and this interplay, the dynamics of interview, must be taken into consideration in any evaluation of the material collected. (1984:956)

A further distortion inevitably takes place when an oral encounter is translated into a written text—which, in our culture at least, assumes a fixed state suggestive of a resolution, a conclusion. As a result, most anthropological life histories and oral historical documents read as if "the narrator is addressing the Cosmos" (Crapanzano 1984:958). But, in fact, it must be remembered that the written text is, at best, a snapshot of a dynamic interchange that is itself part of an ongoing relationship between two particular people.

Moreover, both the storyteller and the audience must share in the conventions of acceptable story telling, conventions that may further distort the veracity of the resulting text. It is almost unheard of in anthropology and oral history to treat life histories with the sort of stylistic analysis accorded to "folk tales," but, unless the folk-literary conventions that guide the creative act in a particular social situation are understood, then one falls into the trap of reading the autobiographical text as if it were a universally valid set of factual case notes. Among the points that Crapanzano suggests researchers begin to pay attention to are indigenous notions of authorship, rhetoric, style, and narration technique, including figurative language, allegory, double entendre, humor, irony, "beginnings and endings," conventional silences, suspense, and denouement (1984:957).

The Question of an Appropriate Analytical Model

Crapanzano's challenging conclusion speaks to the familiar question "What's it good for?" If the autobiographies, biographies, life histories, or life stories cannot be "verified" in the absolute and global sense that has traditionally been upheld, why should they continue to be collected? Simply admiring them as vaguely literary products seems inadequate because researchers often have to go to so much trouble to get them in the first place. Crapanzano holds out hope that generalizations can be drawn out of personalized data, just as traditional social scientists believed, but what he calls "dynamic models" must arise from a source other than the text. It was noted above that generalizations might profitably be drawn from techniques by which autobiographers chose to communicate their experience of self to others rather than from the text alone.

In the same spirit, Crapanzano urges a consideration of the "dynamics of the interview in which the life history is, so to speak, invented" (1984:959). The text, he says, "provides us with a conventionalized gloss on a social reality that, from a strict epistemological point of view, we cannot know" (1984:959). We end up, then, by discussing "the dynamics of narration rather than the dynamics of society" (1984:959). But is it possible that the "dynamics of narration" themselves can serve as clues to the "dynamics of society"? And, if so, how can such a study be conducted?

It is my contention that the production and dissemination of autobiographies is a matter of encounters between subjects and audiences, the latter represented first by the scholar directly involved in the collection of the account, and then, more broadly, by the readers/listeners who will share in both the personal narrative text and in the scholar's interpretation thereof. Researchers may therefore fruitfully use some of the insights of the symbolic interactionist approach in order to be able to draw critical generalizations from these encounters.

My approach to interactionism derives from the sociologist Ralph Turner (1968), who notes that cultural definitions of roles are often vague or even contradictory. (An anthropologist might add that this proposition becomes more nearly valid as the society under question becomes larger and more heterogeneous.) At best, the conventional definition of roles provides a general framework for behavior, hardly a detailed checklist of specific options. People thus do not merely "take" roles, as earlier theorists would have it; they make roles in the sense of defining their responses in specific circumstances from among a large repertoire of potentially available behavioral choices. They then communicate to others what roles they are playing.

To be sure, role making does not occur in a vacuum; people still form their ideas about what to do from "role models," and they have the capacity (unless they are psychiatrically disordered) to set aside or modify their choices if they perceive that their "audience" will not accept them. The source of continuity is not in a set of established decisions about acceptable behavior but rather in a repertoire of conventionalized symbolic communicative strategies that enable "actors" in a social drama to manipulate their own and others' roles.

Indeed, people act as if all others in their environment were playing identifiable roles, and they tend to interpret the gestures of others accordingly. People subtly seek to verify their perception that the other person is, in fact, playing the same game. There are criteria both internal (does this role facilitate interaction just between us two?) and external (is this role likely to be recognized by reputable others, were they to come upon our interaction?) by which we verify our interactions.

We, of course, begin by making roles that reinforce our self-conception, but may adapt when these roles are not verifiable in a given context. For example, someone with a strong, aggressive self-image might always seek to assume a leadership role. But if that person joins a Quaker meeting, where decisions are made by quiet consensus, the role cannot be sustained. The person has the choice of either abandoning that group or modifying behavior so as to fit in more comfortably. The "audience" is not likely to say, "Hey, stop that offensive behavior!"

We therefore rely on our socialization to enable us to pick up the more subtle cues that give the same message. In this view, socialization does not provide us with a repertoire of settled conclusions but rather with a repertoire of gestures and other communicative techniques, as well as the ability to interpret them. The "culture shock" experienced by researchers doing fieldwork in exotic settings is not really a matter of ignorance about specific customs—anyone can pick up a book and acquire such information. The discomfort arises from the critical inability to interpret symbols of interaction and to respond accordingly.

The situation is similar for an oral historian, for example, collecting a story from an informant. The researcher probably tends to assume that the informant is playing the game as defined and so assumes the role of "interviewer," believing further that the informant will be providing straightforward, "factual" responses to the interview stimuli. The informant may, however, be playing another game, thinking of himself or herself as a storyteller and perceiving the researcher to be an interested audience, a large "grandchild" perhaps. Both can proceed quite happily until the symbolic gestures of one of them serve to convince the other that "something is wrong." The researcher may begin to feel that the informant is "fooling around," or the subject may think that the researcher is rudely impatient. One or both may thus shift behaviors and responses around until both are comfortable again, even if only temporarily.

In their usual anxiety for the factuality of the finished text, researchers generally treat these often fleeting little interactive dramas as irrelevant irritations, when, in fact, they may provide more valuable clues than one realizes. In Turner's view, the very fact that the researcher and informant can recognize each others' cues (even if belatedly) and modify their behaviors without appearing to disturb the surface of their interaction is perhaps more indicative of a stable cultural "core" than any specific factual information that can be exchanged.

When the researcher and informant are of such different cultures that the cues are not recognized at all and the encounter does indeed fall apart, the researcher need not bemoan the failure to obtain a "usable" document. He might review the interaction itself to see what cues the informant was actually trying to convey, whether they are part of that culture's repertoire of narrative techniques (since it is fully possible that the informant was telling the researcher in effect to bug off), and to study the repertoire of appropriate responses.

One advantage held by traditionally trained anthropologists over other types of researchers who go into the field to collect personal documentation is that they will, if at all possible, set up a long-term participant-observation residence in the community under study. In this way, they can begin to internalize the cues of interaction that the researcher whose sole purpose is the generation of texts may miss.

The "cognitive sociologist" Cicourel (1973) proposes three major techniques that guide interaction.

1. If actors sense that ambiguity exists about what is going on, they will emit gestures designed to guide themselves back to a "normal form," or a common ground of role playing. For example, coworkers who engage in a bantering flirtation over coffee may find that they are tending to overstep the line of "business propriety" and enter an emotional relationship that they are not prepared to deal with. So one or both may abruptly start talking about the stock market, or rifle through papers in an attaché case, or glance at a watch, or give some other indication that this is a business meeting after all and not a lovers' tryst.

2. If actors sense that they have very different personalities, backgrounds, or interests and yet are forced into a situation that seems to demand interaction, they will seek out some topic about which they can assume common agreement, if not necessarily real interest (the familiar "talk about the weather" ploy at cocktail parties).

3. Conversations or other interactions are rarely, if ever, "complete." It would be exceedingly tedious for each actor to be absolutely explicit about everything that must be committed. In American English, we are fond of saying, "you know," to fill in gaps in a conversation. The unspoken assumption of a phrase like "Kids! Well, you know . . ." is that the other actor will, in fact, know what's the matter with kids, without the first person engaging in an elaborate disquisition. They can proceed to the particular incident they want to speak about, which is supposedly an illustration of the general problem that remains unarticulated. Only rarely in our culture do people say, "No, I don't know—tell me." Such a response, even if honest and well intended, is likely to be interpreted as rude because it symbolically says, "You and I aren't on the same ground at all—we can't assume that we have verified the roles we're setting up for each other."

The general "rules" seem fairly commonsensical, although there is probably some heuristic value in making explicit that which "everybody knows" but of which they may not be consciously aware. However, Turner prefers to delineate the "main tendency propositions" that may shape our descriptions or interpretations of interactions. Such a proposition is one that takes the form "In most normal situations, X tends to occur." It is not a statement of covariance but a statement of what is presumed typically to transpire in the course of interaction. This propositional inventory is based on the assumption that interaction does not involve simple conformity but rather active construction of reciprocal "lines of conduct" among actors who are in the process of adapting to each other in more or less informal situations. "Interactionism" is basically a study of the ways in which people attempt to give coherent form to informal situations.

Turner's propositional inventory may be summarized for the purpose of this text under six major headings:

1. *Emergence and character of roles.*—People view the roles and seek consistency of behavior by interpreting the behaviors of others as elements of recognized roles.

2. *Role as an interactive framework.*—Roles are defined dyadically, and interaction is regularized by modifying behavior so as to create at least the impression of complementarity.

3. *Role in relation to actor.*—As long as people remain in a social situation, they will continue to be identified by roles they have formerly assumed in that situation, even if their behavior changes. New actors entering that situation will be assigned or will adopt roles consistent with or complementary to ones already established in that setting. The newcomer is usually induced to "go along with the crowd" through the interactive mechanisms that are grouped together and popularly called "peer pressure."

4. *Role in organizational settings.*—Statuses and roles tend to merge in organizational settings more nearly than in informal social settings. Roles in organizational settings (such as "CEO," "supervisor," "secretary") tend to be formalized according to objective canons of behavior rather than in ways shaped by the subjective interaction of specific players.

5. *Role in social settings.*—People have a tendency in

smaller, more intimate interactions to adopt roles that reflect broader social contexts. (For example, a society's definition of an appropriate female role may influence what a woman does when she is first introduced to a man, regardless of his particular personality, values, or expectations.) All people, even in "simple" societies, assume multiple roles, either simultaneously, or over the course of time. But in either case they tend to assume roles that are consistent with each other. People prominent in business or politics in our culture, for example, will probably develop leisure roles that are consistent with "professional dignity," such as golfer or charity volunteer. Such persons would likely not be weekend drivers in a demolition derby, even if that's what they'd really like to be doing. After a time, they may even come to feel that that which they have to do is that which they want to do.

6. *Role and the person.*—People seek to resolve tensions among roles and to avoid contradictions between self-conceptions and the roles they assume. For example, in our culture, many men who are attracted to dance as an art form (still widely considered to be an inappropriate male interest) will formulate elaborate explanations about how the ballet is actually a more exacting form of athletic prowess than football.

Two overall "explanatory propositions" link these "main tendency" propositions: (1) Functionality is the process whereby roles are used to achieve ends or goals in an effective and efficient manner, and (2) a role is viable when the conditions surrounding performance of that role make it possible to play it with some personal reward.

Following are descriptions of four of the author's research projects that have utilized personal narratives of various types and from various sources. Three of these projects have taken the traditional analytical approach of accepting the textual integrity of the narratives as if they were documents of some sort of historical, sociocultural, or psychological reality. These studies are presented so as to demonstrate the limitations of this view, although such analyses are certainly useful in some clearly defined research situations. The fourth project, which makes use of the insights of the symbolic interactionists discussed above, is presented so as to clarify the nature of the encounters that generated the texts in question. I suggest that such an approach is one way to give analytical shape to the position pioneered by Crapanzano.

3 /
Freddie: The Personal Narrative of a Recovering Alcoholic— Autobiography as Case History

IN 1970 THE AUTHOR began a cross-cultural study of alcoholism. The main thesis behind this research was drawn from the "transcultural psychiatric" theory of Alexander Leighton (1959): the several social, political, and economic forces that are linked together and called "modernization" will, to a greater or lesser degree, encourage the social disintegration of traditional communities. That disintegration will, in turn, generate relatively high levels of psychosocial stress, which is a significant risk factor in mental disorder. The emergence of "problem drinking" in a community may be an important symptom of this process.

The investigation took place in Trinidad, an island in the West Indies whose history of colonial mercantilism and plantation economy has left it with an ethnically segmented population. The community that was the focus of the research consisted of persons of Indian descent. Indentured laborers were brought to the West Indian colonies from British India from 1837 until 1917. In Trinidad, they found relative prosperity and stayed on to form a well-entrenched agrarian community. Black Trinidadians, by contrast, preferred to leave the land, the symbol of the hated slave system, and by and large became town people involved in industrial, craft, and professional pursuits. For decades, the two communities had existed side by side on the small island without a great deal of interaction. The Indians had preserved a fair amount of their traditional culture.

But in the decades following World War II and since Trinidad achieved independence in 1961, the political and economic climate changed, and more and more Indians began to move into the mainstream of the island's political and economic life. As they did so, the communal solidarity and cultural traditionalism of the ethnic group began to crack. At the same time, the Indians, descendants of a proudly teetotaling culture, were turning to alcohol in alarming numbers. Even so, Indian alcoholics seemed to be much more willing to seek treatment than problem drinkers of the island's other ethnic groups.

Collecting life histories of Indian alcoholics in Trinidad had been projected as part of the research design. In one sense, collecting such life histories was easy, at least among those in treatment, especially those who were members of Alcoholics Anonymous (AA). A certain confessional style typifies that organization and made many of the recovering alcoholics among my informants eager to tell their stories. I was well aware, of course, of the highly conventionalized nature of AA life stories, a style developed for brief presentations at weekly meetings and structured for maximum impact. These brief stories emphasize one or two specific incidents that demonstrate "how low-down I did sink in the gutter" and highlight the actions of the friend (usually a former drinking partner) who sponsored the speaker into AA. Such stories (and I heard and recorded literally hundreds of them in the course of a year of fieldwork) were major sources of information about AA, its membership, its organizational structure, and the system of values it seeks to impart. Much of the ethnographic information about AA in the Trinidadian context that found its way into the resulting monograph (Angrosino 1974) is underscored by the information conveyed by these brief stories, called "contributions" by the members.

But they were not life histories in any meaningful sense of the term. In their formal consistency, they seemed to obscure, rather than illuminate, the factors that shaped individuals' behavior in the particular cultural context. Except for their specific local details—such as the section of Frederick Street in the capital city, Port of Spain, where drunks like to sleep on the sidewalk—these stories could have been told by recovering alcoholics anywhere. Indeed, certain of the more sophisticated pioneers of the AA movement in Trinidad had adopted a style common in the United States, which they had learned from the

AA literature. Because of their prestige, they were widely imitated by their compatriots on the island. Moreover, AA members' contributions were essentially success-oriented: they were men who, although never cured of their disease, were at least straightening out their lives.

But AA is not, for many cultural and psychological reasons, a vehicle that suits all alcoholics. What about people who were recovering by other means, or who weren't recovering at all and were still members seeking treatment for their illness? And what was the real experience behind the conventional verbiage of the AA members' stock contributions?

Late in the course of my fieldwork, I felt I had achieved enough rapport and had learned enough about the culture in general to be able to sit down at length with informants in and out of AA and collect genuine life histories. Still relatively new to the process of life history collection and needing to leave the field very soon, I was not able to record many usable, complete texts. Some that were produced were appended to the monograph, but they did not form a body of data from which I was confident in drawing generalizations about the process of recovering from alcoholism. They did serve as individual case histories in a traditional, anthropological, life history format.

Freed and Freed review the criteria that distinguish the case history from the life history. They define the former as an organized set of facts bearing on the development of individual subjects and focusing on their psychological and medical history. They note (1985:105), however, that "anthropological techniques used in life histories are employable to reconstruct [a subject's] case history, particularly [the subject's] early years." In the literature on the social dimensions of alcoholism, perhaps the most detailed, longitudinal case history that fits this pattern is that by the sociologist Robert Straus (1974), who conducted fieldwork in the anthropological style.

In the Freeds' view (1985:105), an "anthropological psychomedical case history" should cover the ecological, cultural, psychological, biological, and etiological context of the conditions of a person's life.

The subject that will be discussed here is a middle-aged Trinidad Indian man whom I have called Freddie in published accounts dealing with him (e.g., Angrosino 1986). He has been recovering in AA since 1970. I conducted in-depth interviews with him from then until 1975, during which time he also periodically provided me with samples of a journal he was keeping as well as an occasional essay written about his childhood and family. I continue to be in touch with him, although I have not been conducting formal fieldwork in Trinidad, so I have been able to follow the development of his case. Freddie's life has been dominated by his alcoholism. His uncontrolled drinking spoiled a promising career, of course. Moreover, his later acceptance of the AA program has been a focal point of all his decisions about family, job, and even politics.

Current medical opinion holds that alcoholism is a chronic, progressive disease, like diabetes, to which it is often compared. Like diabetes, it is a disease in which the metabolism of a certain basic substance (in this case ethanol) is impaired, leading to malfunctions of one or more organs or organ systems. Like diabetes, alcoholism can never be cured, although, with monitored maintenance, its effects can be mitigated if caught in time.* Some evidence suggests that members of different ethnic groups metabolize ethanol at different rates and hence are more or less prone to the disease (see, for example, Fenna et al., 1976), but alcoholism as a medical syndrome runs essentially the same course no matter where it is found. But, if the syndrome itself transcends culture, its symptoms do not. After all, the most immediate and obvious manifestation of alcoholism is a change in behavior. Alcoholics say or do things that mark them somehow as not normal, and normality is, in the last analysis, a culture-bound phenomenon.

In their provocative study of drunken comportment, MacAndrew and Edgerton (1967) noted that there is no such thing as a universal alcoholic behavior. Rather, alcoholics are character-

---

* The classic disease concept statement was formulated by Jellinek 1960; see Pattison, Sobell, and Sobell 1977 for a comprehensive review of more recent biomedical thinking about the disease.

ized by whatever behavior seems to violate the approved standards of their culture. In middle-class, work ethic–oriented American society, alcoholics often play a childlike, irresponsible, boisterous "good-time Charlie," but in some aggressively macho Latin American societies they become passive and withdrawn. It thus becomes important to understand the historical and cultural milieu in which the alcoholic lives in order to understand the course of the disease. To be sure, individual psychological processes are also at work, but they interact with the larger milieu to create an alcoholic pattern typical of a given community. For this reason, the anthropological psychomedical case history can serve to illustrate forces that may influence the society at large.

Freddie seems in many ways to be a classic example of a "dependent" personality. Although gifted in many ways (he is a talented singer, an effective public speaker, and a master at his trade of auto mechanics), he has always tended to see himself as weak and stupid and has consequently sought out powerful patrons to bolster his confidence.

The roots of Freddie's psychological makeup may be traced to the circumstances of his birth. His mother, a Muslim (a minority among the Indians who migrated to Trinidad), became pregnant with Freddie as a result of an irregular liaison. The identity of his biological father has never been officially established. Nevertheless, Freddie steadfastly insists that he is a certain locally prominent *zamindar* (Indian plantation overseer), who had, according to the local gossips, made a fortune by selling his employers' crops in a kind of black-market arrangement. Because of his wealth, this man was able to buy off peoples' memories of his shady past, and he died, rich and powerful, not long before I met Freddie. Although fathering an illegitimate child would certainly have been in character for this man, no other clues existed that would have established him as Freddie's father, and he never gave the slightest hint of acknowledging Freddie's existence, let alone a family connection. No one else in the district shared Freddie's convictions, and they chalked up his belief to his alcohol-addled brain. As he tells the story, however, there is not the slightest doubt:

Don't think I don't know what they all say—that is a lie I'm
lying. But as sure as I'm here talkin' to you now that lady got
herself fixed up by that ole son of a bitch. How do I know? Hell,
man—how can a man not recognize his own pappa? We got the
same eyes, the same smile—you just look at his picture and try
to tell me different! And what's more, he knew it too. I could
always tell by the way he looked at me goin' down the
road—like he wanted to reach out and claim me for his own,
take me for a ride in that big car of his. He never did, you know,
but that don't change nothin'. We's still blood-on-blood to each
other.

The mother, disgraced in the eyes of her very traditional family,
fled the scene as soon as the baby was born. She is said to have
gone off to Venezuela with a sailor and only returned as an old
lady, to die in her home village. This return occurred within
months of the "father's" death, a highly significant coincidence
to Freddie. As a matter of fact, though, she lived on for more
than ten years in a little shack at the end of a dirt road leading off
from Freddie's own home into the bush. She had a local reputation as an *obeah* lady—a maker of magic—and when I first
visited the area I was told to avoid her. I did not find out until
nearly a year later that she was Freddie's mother, even though I
had gotten to know him quite well during that time. He had
always spoken of his mother as having died shortly after her
disappearance many years before, and his subsequent relations
with the old lady who lived down the road were frosty and anything but filial.

Freddie was taken in by a couple he calls his "uncle and
aunt," although they were not related to his family. They had
simply taken pity on the dishonored girl and her poor baby.
Because the couple were about to leave the village to take up
residence in Port of Spain, they braved local wrath and accepted
the baby as their foster child. The "uncle" was a Hindu, and his
wife had been converted to the Presbyterian church. Freddie often speaks of his Muslim heritage, however, and ostentatiously
refers to Pakistan, rather than India, as his ancestral homeland.

He ascribes numerous virtues, both physical and moral, to the Muslims. At the same time, he jokingly decries the Hindus for their unprogressive ways and is critical of Christian Indians, who, he feels, have betrayed their culture and basic nature. And yet he was raised in a Hindu-Christian household and is reasonably knowledgeable about both those religions. He also knows very little about Islam and has never lived in accordance with its precepts; he has never made even the slightest attempt to take formal training the religion or to learn anything about Islamic culture, for he assumes he "knows it all in the bones."

Freddie speaks warmly about his "uncle," not so much because of his act of kindness in taking in a foundling but because he was a "man of the world":

> Now my Uncle, he was a fine man, the best I ever knew. He could recite you poetry just like a schoolmaster. He read all the papers and could tell you anything you wanted to know about politicians and them—not like he was preachin', but if you like asked a question, he'd always have the answer. And cars! He knew more about cars than any American, I bet. Yeah, he was a fine man.

During World War II, the U.S. armed forces built a large military base in Trinidad (to protect the Venezuelan oil fields from Nazi submarine sabotage), and young people on the island flocked to work there. The jobs paid well by local standards, and the men learned "modern" trades that would make them highly desirable in the postwar workplace. The Americans impressed the Trinidadians as more easygoing, more full of life, and more tolerant than the reserved and stuffy British to whom they were accustomed. Most of the natives who associated with the Americans were black people, who already spoke English and were acquainted with Euro-American culture.

The Indians, who had kept to themselves for decades, lived in a world apart. Community leaders were not favorably impressed by the freewheeling Americans, and they discouraged young Indian men from being corrupted at the base. But a few made the bold move, Freddie's "uncle" among them. He worked at the base for two or three years, learning to be an auto mechanic, the trade he eventually passed on to his adopted son. Using the money he earned, he bought both a small garage and a bar, the latter designed like an American cocktail lounge (as opposed to an old-fashioned Trinidadian rumshop). It catered to the soldiers from the base during the last year of the war, then to the cruise-ship tourists who visited the island.

Freddie thus grew up with models of gaudy wealth, power, and nonchalant conviviality that were dramatically different from those of the Indian villages. What seems to have impressed him most was that the customers drank Scotch, a drink unheard of in the bush. It seemed inconceivable to him that anyone would ever get drunk on that elegant beverage, the way people he knew got drunk on common rum. The Americans just seemed to get sophisticatedly tipsy, not sloppy and sick. (He admits that he did not follow them back to their rooms to observe their hangovers.) It was a fantasy of the good life that Freddie grew up in. As soon as he was home from school, he headed straight for the bar, where he helped out his "uncle" by washing glasses and sweep-ing up. As he himself now recalls his childhood, "I grew up in a nightclub." He says it with some regret but also with much in the way of pleasurable pride. He sees that childhood as infinitely preferable to that of Indian boys of his own age, stuck in the villages and pulled out of school after only a year or two in order to cut cane. "I know it's a bad thing to say," he admits, "but some times I got to be thankful that my mother got herself in trouble that way."

Freddie's "uncle," under the influence of his Presbyterian wife, was a strict teetotaler, but at the same time he was an indulgent "father" who could not resist Freddie's charming eagerness to "be like an American." That goal meant the youth had to learn to sip Scotch, make interesting and risqué small talk, and impress the ladies. He did not become an alcoholic in any smashingly climactic way. He started off as a dashing young barroom Lothario. "You know, them tourist ladies really liked me, 'cause I looked like somebody out of a movie—I didn't look just like the guys next door. Well, not so much the English ladies—they was always a little standoffish. But the Americans! Oh yes, I was a favorite. I guess they got a little tired of blond guys with blue eyes. They wanted somebody more exotic, and that was me!" But he ended up as a middle-aged man who couldn't stop drinking. Looking back, he said, "How did this thing happen? I kept askin' it myself. I couldn't even look at myself in the mirror—I looked like hell, you know. Oh I still had to put on a bold front—a man's always got to try to impress a lady, even if he's on his death bed—but I knew the game was all over." He couldn't make a living at the garage because his habits had become too irregular, and he was no longer in a condition to support himself on his charm.

He had married a fine, strong-minded woman (also a Presbyterian convert) and had fathered three children by the late 1950s, but his family life was a shambles. There was never any money in the house, and, though he was rarely physically abusive, he was certainly not an attentive husband or father. "That's probably the worst of it all. I had the best little family a man could hope for, and I pissed away all my chances to make them happy like they deserved. But I couldn't see it then."

During this period of decline, his "uncle" died, prompting Freddie to attach himself successively to various "big men," who he hoped would see to his advancement in the world beyond the ramshackle ruins of his fantasy life. He ran errands for a prominent attorney, he chauffeured a patrician doctor from time to time, and did a variety of vaguely described and probably illegal favors for an Indian political boss. These men all liked Freddie because he was bright and knew how to deal with "nice people"—he was not some bumpkin straight off a sugar plantation. But each of these patrons abandoned him as his drinking became more and more of a public embarrassment and his demands for extra money to buy food and clothing for his family more of a nuisance. His most decisive patron, however, came along after he had been fired by the politician:

I was in town (Port of Spain) like usual. But I was crazy

somehow. I was so ashamed and I wanted to be good, and I kept telling people—strangers on the street!—that I was gonna change. They was all avoidin' me, of course. I wasn't even all that drunk, but they thought I musta been crazy or something. Anyway, that's when the Salvation Army preacher spotted me. He came up to me and said if I needed a place to stay the night, he'd help me. You know, I didn't even think about the family—how I'd promised to come home that night with some groceries for a change. I just told the preacher, 'Yeah, I need help,' and off I went with him. He said he'd give me a meal and some pocket money for sweeping up and taking out the trash. He even give me a cot for the night, and all he asked was I stay sober for the night. Well, you must know how I was—people was always sayin' things like that to me, and I'd promise 'em anything and then do what I damn pleased. But this was different. I said, 'OK, whatever you say, chief,' and I meant it. There was just something about him. He just looked to me—oh, how can I say it?—like my uncle. Not looks, I guess—just something about his kindness reminded me of my uncle. Somehow I knew he was really interested in what happened to me.

Through this preacher, Freddie eventually became associated with AA. His sponsor, a reformed drinking buddy, had joined the Salvation Army, and both he and the preacher saw to it that Freddie stayed sober. He was on and off the wagon for more than seven years before he "made it good." It was always his shame at letting down his two patrons rather than guilt at what he was doing to his family that led him back to AA after a "slip."

Through AA, Freddie met an influential industrialist (also a recovering alcoholic) who gave him a good job and has been something of an adopted grandfather to his children and now grandchildren. This man also put up the money that enabled Freddie to buy a small house back in his old country village, where he now lives at some distance from the temptations of the wicked city. Freddie is not unaware of his constant search for a father-figure. "I need some smart guy to put it right for me," he says ruefully. "I can't do nothing for myself—never could —except get myself in the gutter."

Freddie's psychological history does not, however, occur in a vacuum. It must be assessed in the context of the historical experience of Indian culture and community organization in Trinidad. When the Indians first came to the island, they were known as a nondrinking people. The strongest alcoholic concoction known in traditional Indian culture was a mild, fermented toddy made from the sap of a kind of palm. The Indians were not, however, innocent of substance abuse, for they were fond of marijuana, which they called *ganja* and which they either smoked or ingested in its brewed, liquid form (*bhang*). *Ganja* acted as something of an anesthetic. It is said to have had a relaxing effect, and the old-timers on the prewar estates retreated to a common room in the workers' barracks to "turn off" the cares of the day with a communal smoke. *Ganja* was thus a symbol of social solidarity as well as a means to peaceful release.

The British authorities sternly disapproved. Their reaction resulted in part from the pressure of the missionaries, who were appalled at this evidence of "degenerate" drug use. But a large share of their indignation came from the plain economic fact that *ganja* could be grown for nothing in any spare garden plot, and no money could be made from the crop. By contrast, rum, an important by-product of processed sugarcane, brought in healthy revenues. And so, early in the twentieth century, the growing and importing of marijuana were outlawed, and estate workers were often paid in rum, though some were merely issued a ration of the liquor as a kind of bonus.

The Indians appear (in the recollections of contemporary informants, at least) to have used the rum in exactly the same way as they used the *ganja*—as a relaxant, a token of quiet, "laid-back" communality. This image was shattered by the new wartime model of the Americans, whose drinking behavior was outrageous. It wasn't that they drank more than the Indians, but they behaved more boldly and aggressively when they did drink. And, because they had the money and the power and were the exemplars of the good life beyond the decaying old estates, their drunken comportment came to be seen as the symbol of having "made it."

The problem was that, on the one hand, young Indian men felt compelled to make their way into the great world because the old agrarian order was manifestly dying. Even some of the elders grudgingly came to accept the inevitability of change and began to take pride in their sons as they learned new skills and moved more securely with "big people." But, at the same time, to move in those circles was an implicit betrayal of all that the traditional culture stood for. The Indian men were being told to make something of themselves, but they were also being told that the more they did so, the more they were being unfaithful to the ancient and glorious culture that had nurtured them and made them special.

Indians as a group were ill equipped by their culture to play the aggressive, individualistic games of American-style go-getting. Hindu culture in particular is oriented to the group: the family, the village. Individuals who "step out" are not necessarily admired, no matter how lofty their accomplishments. They are deviants who will, in the conventional veiw, come to grief because of their presumptuousness and betrayal of the community.

One of the strongest attractions of AA to the Indians is its focus on the group. One of the clearest principles of the organization is that the alcoholic is weak and can do nothing until this weakness is acknowledged. The weaknesses of all can be pooled into a common source of strength. The rugged individual with a tough ego has no place in AA; one must learn to become a servant of all. This attitude, which might be uncongenial in some cultures, strikes a reassuring note among Indian alcoholics. Freddie, for example, extols the virtues of the AA group, which is just like his old gang of drinking buddies, though their aim now is sobriety. The group that Freddie attends is, in fact, composed mostly of men he drank with. The emphasis on the sponsor is also a typically Indian image; the relationship is not unlike that of a religious novice and his guru.

The tensions in Freddie's life—the uprooted family, the push toward independence and a "modern" model of behavior at war with the yearning for settled verities, the conviction of the unworthy self in constant need of support and assistance—are also to be found in the historical situation of Indian culture as it was transposed to Trinidad. Although Freddie's case history, in all its detail, is highly individual and particular, it is also reflective of the evolution of a culture in a special sociohistorical context. A study of his life thus serves both anthropological and psychological purposes—if we can accept the convention that the details of that story are true and would be conveyed in the same way to anyone asking him to relate it. Did my friendship with Freddie affect the form as well as the content of what he told me? What does friendship mean in Trinidadian Indian culture anyway? These questions, which might have had some impact on the resulting case history, are not ordinarily dealt with in life history research. Crapanzano's account of his relationship with Tuhami and Wilson's with Oscar were not yet published when I first worked with Freddie, and the doubts they raised as to the verifiability of the autobiographical text did not impact my use of his case materials nor my use of other forms of autobiographical data in other projects, which are described in the following pages.

4 /
Albert Gomes: Autobiography as Psychohistory

AUTOBIOGRAPHICAL and biographical materials have contributed significantly to the growth of the field of historical social psychology, more popularly known as psychohistory. Scholars in this field study the "minds, attitudes, systems of orientations, motivations, ways of thinking, patterns of conduct of people in the past periods" as well as "the impact of beliefs, values, ideologies, attitudes and other psychological factors on historical processes" (Szcepanski 1981:226). Two major forms of research have been conducted by scholars who identify themselves as psychohistorians. The first form has been adopted by persons interested in collective representations of personality; they have looked for an explanation of shared personality traits which seem to be found commonly among members of the same culture in understanding child-rearing practices. Since such practices have changed substantially over time, there has been an implicit evolutionary bias in the writings of such scholars as De Mause (1975) and Aries (1965). Anthropologists, however, have been critical of these works because they have focused on historical change within Western civilization and have ignored the wider range of child-rearing practices extant in other cultural traditions.

More immediately relevant to the concerns here is the form of psychohistory that has produced the psychobiography: the analysis of the lives of important historical figures in light of psychological theory. Although psychological phenomena can be studied in many ways, psychohistory has been most closely associated with a clinical approach, and one heavily influenced by psychoanalytic principles at that. For example, Mazlish's study of James and John Stuart Mill (1975) used the concept of the Oedipus complex to explain the relations between father and son, a relationship that he depicts as paradigmatic of intergenerational relationships in western European culture in the nineteenth century. Mazlish's point is that a particular constellation of circumstances—the Industrial Revolution and its concomitant political and economic upheavals—set the stage for a particularly vivid "generation gap." The uncertainties of the era seem to have stimulated increased patterns of oral dependence and depression. Similarly, Loewenberg (1971) has studied autobiographies from the cohort of Germans who came of age around the time of World War I, persons who suffered the privations of the war and the humiliation of defeat and became prime recruits for the Nazi movement. The economic dislocation and political humiliation they experienced created a set of strongly felt tendencies toward frustration, hatred, and violence. The absence of fathers who went off to fight the war and anger against those same fathers who had lost the war stimulated a particularly virulent form of Oedipal conflict. Traditional German adherence to the strong father was thereby undermined, but the attendant focus on the mother (who held the family together) raised the unacceptable specter of latent homosexuality. These various feelings were resolved by acceptance of Hitler (a "big brother" rather than a "father") and by immersion in the symbols of violence and power associated with Nazism. This psychoanalytic orientation has often led to accusations that psychohistorians improperly put historical figures "on the couch" and analyze their psyches long after the subjects are dead and in no position to speak for themselves. Although there has been a certain amount of exaggeration (and perhaps even sensationalizing) of the method, particularly in works addressed to commercial audiences, the general approach is nevertheless potentially useful for students of the personal dynamics involved in social history.

The psychohistorian, like the clinician, is involved in the selection of experiences from the lives of subjects, fragments that are then "restored to intelligibility" in such a way that the life is, in effect, "ordered into an interpretation" (Prisco 1980:28). A potential source of abuse is the utilization of any biographical data that come to hand when reconstructing the life of a historical figure. The modern, scientific tendency is to aim for factual completeness. But, as clinicians well know, not all of a subject's life experiences are equally important, and experiences that in retrospect seem to have been important are sometimes seized upon as focal points of a psychoanalytic analysis, even if in reality they were psychologically inconsequential.

For this reason, psychohistory tends to work best when autobiographies are available. Although they can be spotty and are sometimes the products of quite deliberate distortions (as pointed out in chapter 2), at least they represent the distortions, omissions, or emphases that the subject personally chose. They are thus more nearly akin to the discoveries a clinician makes than are the "complete lives" reconstructed from a variety of sources.

Yet the use of autobiography creates a limitation on the kind of analysis that can be performed because writers of autobiography are usually persons of extraordinary accomplishment: political leaders, artists, philosophers. The interior life of "common" people of past eras is largely closed to the psychohistorian. Although even the most transcendent geniuses are still, in some ways, a product of their time, there is little justification for assuming that they were in any way "typical" of their eras. And yet, as Wilson has cogently noted (1974:x), in the lives of extraordinary people "there is . . . the exaggeration of what passes unnoticed, though not unsuffered, in the lives of ordinary people." Psychohistory must therefore deal with these historical superstars in a very different way from that of the oral historian collecting the life histories of otherwise anonymous "folk." The analysis of the autobiography of an extraordinary person must stress the general tendencies of that life, as distinct from the analysis of the case history, which stresses the particular.

Perhaps the most widely cited theoretician of the psychohistorical approach is the psychoanalyst Erik Erikson, whose well-known studies of Luther (1958), Gandhi (1969), and Hitler (1963:326–58) have helped create a framework for dealing with extraordinary subjects. Erikson's approach is predicated on an extension of basic Freudian principles. Whereas Freud saw the fundamental traumas that determine the personality as products of the conflicts of early childhood, Erikson has viewed the development of the personality as a lifelong process. His is thus an optimistic reversal of the somewhat gloomy Freudian view of toilet-training-as-destiny; conflicts of later life can yield positive outcomes even if negative results were experienced earlier on. Moreover, Erikson is concerned not only with the unfolding of personality but also with the evolution of character, the moral, self-conscious side of behavior. The aim of life, he contends, is to become not only a "whole" person but also a "virtuous" one, referring to the word *virtue* in its original sense of "strength" (see Erikson 1963). His view is consonant with the interactionist perspective delineated in chapter 6 in that life is a series of critical encounters, which are inherently conflictual and provide the raw material for growth and change. Eriksonian personality is not a determinate entity as it is for Freud; it is a process of developmental growth that ends only with death.

Erikson has wedded his developmental analytic framework to the study of autobiographical materials in a psychohistorical vein. It is not surprising that in doing so he focuses on decisive conflicts in the life of a subject rather than on mere events or experiences. His developmental scheme posits eight steps, each one typified by a conflict. In his psychohistorical works, the most critical of these stages has turned out to be the fifth, which occurs normally at the time of adolescence and is a conflict between identity and role confusion (Erikson 1968). The adolescent ego needs and seeks out continuity in the midst of changing physical attributes. At the same time, the onset of maturity also requires a standard of adult behavior, because adolescents are not yet sufficiently self-confident to do their own thing. Hence, they seek the comfort of the group. They must go beyond their families for this support inasmuch as the family is identified with their childhoods, which they seek symbolically to overcome. The adolescent peer group, unsure of its own values, usually adopts some larger ideology to ensure conformity and to rationalize behavior. In our own day, this ideology often derives from the attitude of rock stars and other media celebrities, although it can be, and often has been, more explicitly political.

This adolescent identity crisis can result in the individual being frozen into an antisocial role. On the positive side, however, the conflict can encourage in the young person a strong sense of ethics, commitment to values, and well-defined personal affiliations (Prisco 1980:19).

Somewhat later in life (typically in middle age), individuals develop a need to work to their potential and, in so doing, to provide guidelines for the next generation. If this need is frustrated, individuals sense that they are stagnating and may question previous career choices and even start on a new career direction (Prisco 1980:1). This process is known as a "generativity crisis." The key to Erikson's psychohistory is his assumption that "a prolonged identity crisis may lead to a generativity crisis . . . in which the individual accepts the concerns of a whole communal body as his own" (Prisco 1980:32).

In essence, the extraordinary historical figure is one who shares the same basic conflicts of ordinary people but who somehow is able to communicate to them the belief that the resolutions he or she has made are efficacious for all of them. Such a person becomes a leader in politics or the arts not so much by transcending the common concerns of the group but by symbolically embodying them in such a way that humbler folk can sense a vicarious resolution (see Erikson 1975).

It must be kept in mind that Erikson's scheme, like Freud's, evolved essentially from observations of clinical populations in Western societies, although both models have been asserted to be universally applicable. Few researchers who have worked in other cultures would accept such a global developmental model, but, for purposes of this discussion, one may assume that human beings in all cultures develop their personalities interactively throughout their lifetime and that certain categories of conflict are instrumental in moving that process along. The specific details that constitute those conflicts will, however, be factors of the local culture.

The research described in chapter 3 was conducted in the culturally plural polity of postcolonial Trinidad. Although that research focused on a specific psychomedical problem within only one segment of the population, I could not but be concerned with the nature of the polity generally, which was the background against which the Indians' particular conflicts were played out. The British had left a core of political institutions to independent Trinidad (a system of government that has proven to be remarkably enduring, one might add), but the various ethnic strands of the population had never integrated completely into a single cultural tradition. The institutions provided a bedrock of stability, but the political culture has always been a swirl of factions and subfactions characterized by "doctor politics"—political leadership based on the sometimes transient coalitions built by charismatic leaders. One effective way to understand this highly personalized political system is by way of the political autobiography.

This chapter applies the Eriksonian analysis to one such autobiography (Angrosino 1976), that of Albert Gomes (1974), who published his memoirs from self-imposed exile in England during the years of my research on Trinidad.* He rose to prominence in the labor movement of the 1930s, a power base that was an important forerunner of nationalist-independence sentiment in Trinidad, as it was throughout the West Indies. He gained a position of influence in the political apparatus that oversaw the transition from colonial to independent status in the 1940s and 1950s and was a leading figure in the establishment of the nobly conceived but ill-fated West Indies Federation. When the federation collapsed and the islands opted for separate independent status, he was derided as a prophet of the old order and his political career was finished. Unable to live in an independent Trinidad from whose political life he was excluded, he sought refuge in the metropole.

Perhaps the most salient feature of Gomes's political adventures is his ethnicity. Colonial Trinidad was often stereotyped as a study in black and white, and the postindependence period has been largely a story of black versus Indian rivalry. But, in addition to the Indian indenture, which proved to be by far the

---

* The following section is taken, with some modification, from Angrosino 1976: 144–53.

most successful such venture, there were other, smaller schemes
of labor importation that resulted in the extreme ethnic heterogeneity of the island today. The title of Gomes's autobiography,
Through a Maze of Colour, reflects this ethnic heterogeneity and
the frustrations it presents for politicians trying to build a
consensus. His ancestral family was from Portuguese Madeira;
like most of the Trinidadian Portuguese, his immediate family
was of the urban, commercial middle class.

Through a Maze of Colour begins not with Gomes's childhood reminiscences but with a highly romanticized account of
his family's history. He states that his maternal grandfather was
abandoned on the doorstep of a Madeiran orphanage, hence the
family name De Cambra ("of the orphanage"). This undeniably
good tale provides a vivid opening to the memoirs, but Gomes's
purpose probably transcends the literary. In the Trinidadian
context, the Indians, Chinese, Portuguese, and Syrian communities have always stressed the psychological advantage they felt
over the black majority, the fact that they could all look back to
substantial cultural traditions that gave substance and meaning to
their ethnicity. The blacks were uprooted and their African cultural traditions suppressed to such an extent that, until the advent
of the Black Power movement in the early 1970s, Africa was a
source of shame more than of pride. But Gomes chooses to intro-
duce himself by stressing his own rootlessness (1974:3):

> My maternal grandfather having been a foundling, a main branch
> of the tree has been abruptly cut off at that point, leaving me free
> to speculate, as vanity or convenience might determine, whether
> prince, rogue or ordinary seducer set in motion the dramatic
> incidents that must have preceded the abandonment of my poor,
> hapless grandparent on the doorstep of an orphanage in Madeira
> many years ago.

Gomes is also at pains to separate himself from his ethnic
group in Trinidad, one that has taken pride in its economic
success but which he despises for its smug satisfaction in the
grossly material side of bourgeois virtue (1974:11):

They were a robust lot, these immigrants from Madeira. They possessed all the animal cunning, concupiscence and penchant for the obscene of the peasant. Their manners were appalling and their general deportment almost totally lacking in the graces of restraint or refinement. Much of what they said and did in public, wise custom reserves for the lavatory or bedroom. All their appetites were large and unrestrained, a misfortune for both their health and morals.

Of Gomes's own childhood, there is hardly a word, and only rather brief, dismissive mention of his father, a somewhat vague figure who was preoccupied with his shop ledgers. However, considerable space in these early chapters is devoted to the mother, whom Gomes remembers as her husband's backbone, the brains behind his business success, and the guiding light of the family's fortunes. The portrait of the mother is highlighted by Gomes's accent on her lower-class origins, which, he feels, gave strength and substance to her later rise to middle-class status. Although he has nothing but contempt for the "peasant" background of the Portuguese in general, he waxes lyrical about his mother's peasant roots (1974:4):

She always preferred the society of her poor Negro friends, and never spoke of the days of her youth and of her friends of that period without warmth and tenderness. She never really lost touch with them. . . . This quality in her extended even to food; it was the native dishes that had been part of the folklore of her past that she most relished and was always wanting; and often she would retrace her footsteps along the path of her recent social advance, about which she was really indifferent, to spend a few quiet hours eating a meal with an old friend in some ramshackle ajoupa [shack] at the periphery of the town.

In strictly "factual" terms, this childhood portrait is glaringly incomplete, but it fulfills an important function in the Eriksonian framework. If Gomes, the product of a small and relatively privileged minority, is ever going to make a case for the value of his leadership, he must broaden his base of identification. And so who he "really" is turns out to be symbolically less important than the image he has created for himself. In a society destined to be dominated by a majority segment that believed itself to be composed of deracinated sojourners, he made himself rootless. In a polity suspicious of the material success of his own group, he expressed his contempt for that group and turned his back on the mercantile values that made it successful. In a confrontation that was to pit the colonial underclasses against the last vestiges of imperial privilege, he deliberately placed himself on the side of the lowly and dispossessed.

Gomes's self-reinvention works on an even more subtle, psychological level as well. One distinctive feature of black family life in the West Indies has been the emphasis on the maternal figure. In part, this kind of emotional matrifocality was the result of an economic system that forced many men to seek employment away from the home area, leaving the job of child rearing to women and their mothers. Moreover, the culture of the lower classes (largely, although not exclusively, black) placed no particular stigma on bearing children out of wedlock. In fact, an important sign of a man's prowess was the siring of many children, whom he was not necessarily obliged to help raise. Children, therefore, were far more apt to establish a close bond with the mother rather than with the father. None of these conditions was operative in the staunchly middle-class and patriarchal Portuguese community of Gomes's youth. Yet in his autobiography he carefully selects and edits his reminiscences in such a way as to yield an image that looks suspiciously like a lower-class black family. Even his romantic tale of the orphaned grandfather is about the maternal, not the paternal ancestor.

Once it establishes his oneness with the masses, Gomes's autobiography proceeds to a section that can be read in Eriksonian terms as an account of an adolescent identity crisis—although, in this case, the event occurred when he was in his twenties. The nature of the conflict is such that Gomes is able to present himself as a paradigm of West Indian youth struggling to establish its identity. It is not only a specifically generational conflict (the standard adolescent rebellion against parental authority) but also, in the context, an image of the rising of colonial underlings against the feeble, decadent imperial regime. The themes of Gomes's identity crisis echo throughout his subsequent political career.

Wilson (1973) has provided what is probably the most cogent analysis of this typical West Indian crisis of identity, which revolves around antithetical concepts labeled "respectability" and "reputation." Respectability is the sum total of the standards imported from the metropole (for example, monogamous marriage, membership in an "acceptable" church, having a fine house, getting a white-collar job); the indigenous elite that succeeded the departed white colonialists would be no less strict than the latter in upholding the sanctity of these standards. No rise in social position is possible without adherence to most, if not all, of the standards of respectability. Reputation, by contrast, is that complex of behaviors that adds up to a person's position within the peer group. For a man, behavior has traditionally included the fathering of many children, oratorical or storytelling ability, and the capacity for drinking large quantities of rum. In short, to have a reputation is to be a "man among men."

The values of respectability and reputation are often contradictory, and people, in frustration, usually end up opting for one or the other rather than trying to achieve or maintain both. The irony for the person who seeks leadership is that, in order to be taken seriously in that capacity, he (it has usually been a "he" in West Indian politics) must be respectable, but yet the respectable man eventually loses touch with the people. Caribbean political and artistic history is full of men of major potential who outgrew the island reputation system and ended up in self-imposed exile in the metropole.

Gomes began in respectability, but, as his autobiography demonstrates, his political trajectory was guided by his need to establish his reputation—an attempt that was doomed to fail from the beginning. Even that failure, however, as indicated above, is paradigmatic of the condition of West Indian leadership. The linchpin of the reputation system is the male peer group. Often this group (called a *lime* in Trinidad) engages in nothing more substantial than street-corner idling. Gomes went away to the United States for a period of study (an experience about which he says nothing in his memoirs); when he returned in 1930, he took up with a circle of young men who were determined to bring "culture" to their island backwater. The group coalesced around the poet Alfred Mendes (also a Portuguese), and it eventually included the "byronic," alcoholic, homosexual poet-politician Tony De Boissiere and the noted essayist C. L. R. James. These men formed a pretentious, muckraking newspaper, the *Beacon,* which was underwritten by the elder Gomes at the urging of his wife. Despite the heavy intellectual pretensions of the *Beacon* group, it remained essentially a Trinidadian *lime,* which is precisely what the younger Gomes wanted:

> Our group preserved its essentially informal character throughout. For this I must claim some credit. I find that people react much more naturally and give much more of their true selves, their talents and idiosyncrasies, when they are not contained in any formal social crucible, especially one of the kind that gives importance to rules of parliamentary procedure. . . . Hence my insistence, throughout the life of our group, that we should eschew chairmen and standing orders and all other aspects of the paraphernalia by which men impose controls upon themselves when they become committees. We met at each other's homes and never around a table, except, of course, one on which there were bottles and glasses. (1974:22–23)

During its brief life, the *Beacon* attracted more than its share of public controversy, numbering the churches as well as the government among its principal antagonists. It ceased publication in 1933, and the group drifted apart. At this point, the elder Gomes purchased a rundown pharmacy in a shabby part of town for his rebel journalist son to run. For the next four years, he did so, feeling like a "classic case of the square peg being forced into the round hole" (1974:27)—his father's pretensions to respectability fighting against his own drive to reassert his reputation, which had been threatened by his father's lack of confidence in continuing to subsidize the *Beacon* group.

Nevertheless, the "intolerable drudgery" of the pharmacy provided Gomes with "a window through which I could hear the murmurs of popular discontent" (1974:27). There he witnessed firsthand the struggles and the miseries of his poor clientele. Realizing the folly of the *Beacon* group, which, in its middle-class way, was preoccupied with "the state of the arts," Gomes learned that the common people had other problems in mind:

> Since I am essentially a product of the mystique [of the middle class], I know the extent to which its fantasies and foibles then constrained me to a romantic approach to the social harshness that surrounded me. Poverty is quite as bad as you imagined when you get to know it, but the mere fact of being with it imparts a certain aplomb which imagination could not possibly provide. Perhaps that is why the middle-class conscience tends to be either overwrought or too condescending in its responses: imagination does not easily get beneath the other fellow's skin. The other reason—and certainly the more fundamental one—is that encapsulation of class is much more hermetic than we are consciously aware. Through the window of the pharmacy I only saw, I did not experience. But I observed enough in the end to persuade me that I could no longer feed my conscience on a diet of verbal protests, and that I could only be at peace with myself—as far as this is possible to any of us—if I acted. But less generous motives also impelled me. I yearned passionately to be at the center of things. (1974:27–28)

He finally got his wish when the upheavals of 1937, a year of widespread labor unrest, propelled him into public affairs.

During this same period, Gomes was married, although he never once mentions by name the helpmate who has been with him through ups and downs ever since, nor is she ever referred to except in passing, as a kind of interested bystander to his adventures. Mrs. Gomes has evidently been a kind of den mother to Gomes's political circle since the 1930s because their various residences have become semiofficial party headquarters over the years. Yet neither she nor their children ever emerge from the shadows in his autobiography. Here again is a reaffirmation of a West Indian pattern of reputability: the tendency to treat the "good woman" to whom one is married as nothing more than an adjunct to one's own activities in the world of men, where all the important things happen. This attitude is especially revealing in contrast to Gomes's treatment of his mother.

The relegation of the wife to the background also contrasts sharply with the treatment accorded to Gomes's longtime colleague in the labor movement and the closest of his political collaborators, Quintin O'Connor. Although never as flamboyantly public a figure as Gomes, O'Connor is credited by many labor insiders in Trinidad as being a major figure in the establishment of the unions on the island. Yet as Brinsley Samaroo notes in his introduction to Gomes's memoirs, "Quintin O'Connor never really comes to life in the work; he is at best at the outer parameters of the struggle" (1974:xvi). This lapse is, in strictly historical terms, quite unfortunate, but from the Eriksonian point of view it is quite revealing. Although O'Connor may not emerge as a character in his own right, he is identified, and his relationship to Gomes is always clear. He is like the "partner" in one's *lime,* the man one hangs out with most frequently. In such relationships one man is typically the strong personality, who faces the outside world, while the other is his sounding board. As such, Gomes and O'Connor are one personage: Gomes the public activist, O'Connor the quiet theoretician and behind-the-scenes diplomat. This quintessential form of Trinidadian friendship behavior is, as Gomes unconsciously shows, a far more emotionally decisive bond—and a far more direct spur to meaningful social action—than is the conjugal bond.

Gomes's eventual entry into public life came as the result of his newfound feeling for "the people," who had demonstrated their profound dissatisfaction with the old order during the tumultuous oil field riots and related activities of 1937. These events forced the colonial government to pay more heed to local concerns and marked the beginning of the process of decolonization and preparation for independence. This turning-point aspect of the riots may not have been as clear at the time as it is in retrospect, but they definitely persuaded Gomes to run for the Port of Spain municipal council in 1938. He paints an amusing portrait of the canvassing techniques of those days. He lost the election because, he implies, he refused to bribe the voters as his opponents were in the habit of doing. Several months later, he was the victor in a special off-term election, although he is discreetly silent about whether he changed his tactics to match those of his rivals.

He almost immediately set himself up as the leading opponent to Trinidad's most influential political figure, the legendary Captain Cipriani. It is almost too tempting to see Gomes's political emergence in metaphorically Oedipal terms. However, just as entering public life in the first place was a means to escape his father's plans, once in the public arena he devoted himself to challenging the great political father figure of his generation. Cipriani, however, was no Milquetoast merchant; although his denunciation of the oil field rebels of 1937 had seriously compromised his political leadership, he was still virtually the only Trinidadian in government who had the ear of the colonial administration.

Gomes's challenge to Cipriani's leadership may seem indirect in strictly historical terms because it was not simply played out in the legislative arena, in which both were active. It was, however, startlingly apt in sociocultural terms. Cipriani had come to represent the established order, and, despite the populist aura of his younger days, he seemed by the late 1930s to be one of the rare men to have come up from the masses to a position of authority, as "respectable" a spokesman for the colony as was to be found. In contrast, Gomes's middle-class background and his fame as an intellectual dilettante had already made him quite respectable. Yet the essence of the colonial identity crisis is that the fully respectable individual must, by definition, establish himself elsewhere, probably in the metropole, because, if one becomes totally respectable, he can no longer function in terms of the reputation system of West Indian society.

Gomes therefore challenged the upwardly rising Cipriani by descending downward, into the masses, as if to say that he was not interested in escaping to the metropole—he wanted to be a "man among men" right where he was. To do so, he championed the trade union movement and devoted his (and O'Connor's) considerable energies and talents to shaping the disorganized popular movement into a real political force.

Unfortunately for Gomes, no matter how a reputable person strives to become respectable, he will likely be dragged down by his jealous fellows. Conversely, no matter how much a respectable person tries to be reputable, they will always push him upwards in their pursuit of vicarious glorification. The two value clusters thus constantly clash, and the polity is constantly in motion. Gomes's very success as the trade union champion pushed him into the highest councils of government. He was elected to the islandwide legislative council and finally was appointed to the governor's figurehead executive committee.

In those capacities, Gomes, only a few years after he had neutralized Cipriani, had himself become the establishment's point man, a shift best illustrated by his break with O'Connor. The latter remained involved with the unions, but Gomes, as a member of the government, had the portfolios of industry and commerce and needed to deal with the capitalists as well as the workers. O'Connor gave up on him. Gomes characterizes the break as inevitable but painful (1974:49)—inevitable because his new job was to attract industry to Trinidad so as to create new employment (and thus he had to tell his union comrades to "cool it" in their demands), painful because it meant the demise of a strong friendship. In the end, though, Gomes, like so many West Indians who have been marked as respectable, opted permanently for respectability rather than reputation.

Although Gomes's career went from "strength to strength," as the Trinidadians say, his power was first compromised by this break with O'Connor and his union base. It was the beginning of the end, albeit the end did not occur for nearly two decades. During the next decade, Gomes, as the minister of labour, industry, and commerce, traveled to Europe and North America on trade missions and related activities. However, he is at pains to characterize his participation in these eminently respectable endeavors as that of the maverick, the "rebel journalist" as aging Peck's bad boy:

> I was determined not to yield, although I was eager to return home, and was under pressure of some members of my delegation to do so. . . . However, when all seemed finally lost, an incident changed the prospect suddenly and brought us victory. Mr. Webb, the Minister of Food, in answering a Parliamentary question, gave some inaccurate information. Our agitation had subsided in anticlimax; but I thought that this might be my chance to effect a revival that would embarrass both Mr. Webb and Mr. Griffiths—and their colleagues. So I waited my chance, and, at what obviously was meant to be a final meeting with our hosts, at which they would politely bid us bon voyage before sending us back home empty-handed, I offhandedly introduced both question and answer, and with an air of offended innocence suggested that the many inaccuracies contained in Mr. Webb's reply left me with no alternative but to disavow them publicly. . . . The immediate reaction convinced me that my barb had found its mark. (1974:140–41)

> I just blew up. I rose to my feet and aggressively declared that it was my intention to withdraw my delegation and to state publicly my reasons for doing so to both the United Kingdom and the West Indian press. I followed this up with a long and impassioned speech in which I charged the Colonial Office with bad faith. I accused them of having brought us to London on pretenses . . . I had relied on my little blackmail which I have never known to fail on such occasions. (1974:146)

And, during the fight to organize the West Indies Federation, in the 1950s, "I categorically refused to be bound by decisions of the Caribbean Labour Congress and became the enfant terrible of their deliberations, which were really no more than wrecking operations somewhat thinly disguised. As a result their main purpose was thwarted" (1974:194).

The clamoring for attention, the reliance on crowd-sweeping oratory, the grandiloquent gesture, the involvement with the "little us" against the "big them" are all the marks of a man among men. Yet they were all being performed by an eminently respectable man in an arena in which such gestures were no longer appropriate. By ironic paradox, Gomes's initial successes had pushed him beyond the confines of the Trinidadian polity, but so desperate was his desire to remain within it and find some identification therein that he continued to behave in reference to the local peer group system even when he was no longer expected to do so. As a result, his putative peers in both respectability and reputation circles drifted away from him.

The formation of the West Indian Federation, a turning point for an entire generation of West Indian politicians, proved to be the last straw for Gomes's long career in public service. The idea behind the federation of the former British territories was, from the British point of view at least, to achieve decolonization painlessly, while preserving a large union that would be economically and politically more viable than a host of island microstates. It was also, no doubt, a means by which Britain could maintain her influence even after independence.

But the federation seemed doomed from the beginning by parochialism. During more than 300 years of West Indian colonialism, anything beyond an island identification had never existed. Even on some tiny islands, people often identified with an estate or district, not the whole island. Some of the larger islands, like Jamaica and Trinidad (and the huge mainland territory of British Guiana) were probably capable of making the transition, but the smaller ones were not. The small islands also grew jealous of the big islands, which seemed destined to dominate the federation and yearned for total independence. British Guiana (now Guyana) withdrew first, taking with it the promise of vast continental acreage that could have been accessible for surplus island populations. It was followed by Jamaica, after an embarrassing referendum defeat for its profederation leaders.

Gomes fervently believed that the federation would be the

salvation of the islands once the British left, but in taking such a stand he was setting himself against powerful countervailing forces of island nationalism. It would be absurd to characterize his faith in the federation as an extension of his Trinidadian dependence on a *lime,* but the notion of solidarity, implicit in the *lime* structure, is not at all a farfetched factor in his attitude.

To understand this problem, it is necessary to look closely at the most intriguing and puzzling chapter of his autobiography, entitled "A Clash of Cultures." Although the bulk of the book is a brisk narrative account of his activities and a clear-eyed analysis of his career and his contemporaries, this chapter reads like a literary exercise. He seems intent on defining a distinctive West Indian culture—a dificult task for an intellectual from a colonial backwater who had grown up thinking that the only relevant culture was that of the metropole. His efforts in this direction are not at all dissimilar to those of many other artists—and not a few nationalist politicians. What is different is that, long before it became fashionable to do so, he was talking about a Caribbean culture, not just a Trinidadian culture. Moreover, his identification of the essence of that culture reflects his romantic identification with the African as well as his rejection of the contribution of the other ethnic strands of the population. The key to this chapter is his discussion of the Shouter sect, an African-inspired evangelical group that had been subject to persecution from time to time. His defense of the sect had made him one of its great heroes, although he was never formally a member. His infatuation with the sect, however, goes far beyond a concern for its legal rights:

> My mother used regularly to employ a nubile Negress to polish our furniture. In those days this was an accepted vocation. . . . This particular young woman belonged to the Roman Catholic faith and was very devout. Indeed, in our household we thought of her always as someone whose personality conveyed an impression of pious restraint. . . . Unconsciously perhaps we were dignifying the quality of "knowing one's place" which we assumed her punctilious exterior to radiate. But when I saw her

writhing in sensual torment to the violent rhythm of the
"Shango" drums she was transfigured. It seemed as if some
magic had been released from her loins that now suffused her
entire being, impregnating every muscle and nerve of her body
with its ecstatic pulsation. And when eventually she fell to the
ground and lay there, fluttering like a chicken with a severed
head, a ripple of terror ran through my blood. The presence of
Roman Catholic icons in a niche directly above her served only
to reinforce the weird character of the scene.

I like to think of that scene as symbolic of the cultural
schizophrenia that all West Indians suffer, not only those who
must reconcile their African . . . past with the Anglo-Saxon influences of the kind of colonialism they have known but European-
oriented ones like myself whose extraterritorial equipment is
even much less dependable. (1974:80)

Gomes's involvement is passionate, sensual. As he had noted
earlier:

I confess to being impatient of the hypocrisy that overlays so
many of our moral judgments. The illusion of virginity may,
after all, be preserved in a scientific study by the application of a
little expertise. . . . But virtue might have been no more intact. I
said as much to my companion, and we debated briskly, she ap-
peared to agree with me eventually that English and West Indian
viewed this matter from quite different points of view, mores,
and temperaments. (1974:75)

Considering the fact that he had already castigated the Portuguese for their concupiscence, it can be no accident that his
celebration of black sensuality occupies the bulk of a lengthy
chapter. He seems to be setting up a kind of ideal typology, of
admirable black sensuality versus viciously hypocritical white
uptightness. This viewpoint is, of course, already something of a
cliché (although it may not have been so among genteel West
Indians of Gomes's generation) and is of interest in this context
only because of his own ambiguous racial status. In Trinidad, the

Portuguese are considered white, but in Britain he was treated as a colored from the colonies. As a white man in Trinidad, he is constrained to reject the sensuality of his own ethnic group because it compromises his respectability, but as a colored from the colonies in the metropole, he celebrates the freedom of blackness as the unhypocritical birthright of a man among men.

It is in this light that his reaction to the federation must be interpreted. A Portuguese, he says, is "the odd man out, the conspicuous cuckoo in the West Indian political nest" (1974:168). Rejecting identification solely as a Portuguese (because of the limitations of such an identity), he must, if he is to have any identity at all, any reputation in the wider sense, identify with a larger group. But, despite his romantic attachment to black culture, he knows he can never be fully reputable in that particular arena because he has already, by the facts of birth and political position, been marked as too respectable. So he looks for better things—not in the totally respectable society of England at first, but in the even more heterogeneous West Indies Federation, in which his peculiarities could be averaged out.

If there are any villains in Gomes's generally genial reminiscences, it is the Indians. Although it was black politicians who engineered his downfall, his romantic attachment to the blacks prevents him from being harsh with them as a group. But the Indians, smug in their "ancient heritage" and ethnic exclusivity, had no such saving grace as free sensuality. Gomes smirks at their adoption of Gandhi caps and saris after India's independence, and he decries their political wavering during the federation years. The Indians, he implies, have achieved both respectability and reputation on their own terms (a highly debatable proposition) and have shut him out even more than have the blacks. Their refusal to assimilate is seen as willful and destructive, and hence reprehensible, as opposed to the occasionally more violent black racialism, which did not become ideological until well after Gomes's career was ended.

The crowning irony of this situation is that Gomes's political eclipse came at the hands of that most respectable of West Indian political eminences, Dr. Eric Williams. Just as Gomes himself had outmaneuvered Cipriani by being a "man among men" (despite the fact that, in terms of social class, he was as respectable as his opponent, if not more so), so Williams outmaneuvered Gomes by playing on popular sentiment and painting his opponent as too much a part of the established order to be an effective postindependence leader. Defeated for election to the Federal Parliament and cut adrift when Trinidad pulled out of the federation to become independent, Gomes moved his family permanently to England. He had earlier relocated from "gay, smelly, proletarian Belmont [a working-class district of Port of Spain]" (1974:166) and settled in Maraval, an elegant section of town, because he feared reprisals from his political enemies. But, as he says, he left his heart in Belmont, and the physical exile in England was merely the affirmation of that earlier spiritual exile.

In summary, then, Gomes's personal adolescent identity crisis (his need to break away from his father and the bourgeois values he represented) impelled him to join a peer group fighting that same battle at the level of the old colonial order inexorably evolving toward independence. His own personal need to prove himself a man among men enabled him to play the role of the wily politician, able to join in the establishment's game and yet promote his personal victory as if it were won for the common people as a whole. He therefore took a crisis that affected most people and turned it into a public drama. Even after he had been pushed off the stage, as it were, he continued to dramatize his struggle by means of his autobiography.

Despite the limitations, both analytical and methodological, of the psychohistorical approach, it can still be a useful means of understanding the ways in which large public events and private, inner conflicts can mesh to shape the affairs of a society.

5 /
Personal Narratives from Aruba: Collective Reflections as Oral Ethnography

A KEY FACT of the political-economic life of the postindependence Caribbean islands has been their differential development. Some islands (for example, Trinidad, Aruba, and Curaçao) have built thriving industrial sectors,* but others have remained tied to declining, monocrop, agrarian economies. The latter have become exporters of labor and often survive on the remittances of citizens working abroad. Although most of the expatriate labor force has traditionally emigrated to the United States, Canada, or Europe, a sizable number of migrants have chosen to move to the more prosperous parts of the Caribbean itself. The insularity of its society, which has for centuries been a psychological as well as a literal geographic fact of life, is therefore breaking down as the islands engage in a complex labor exchange.

This process can be studied from any number of social science perspectives, but the personalistic view should not be neglected when analyzing large-scale political-economic issues. The study of narratives collected from persons involved in the process of change can thus be a useful adjunct to a more quantifiable economic survey.

The research project to be discussed here had its roots in a study on the island of Saba, in which the author participated as a graduate student. The smallest of the Dutch islands, Saba has historically been the most isolated. It has always been an exporter of labor, and its men have been highly valued in the various seafaring trades throughout the Caribbean and the United States.

---

* To the extent that these industrial sectors were built around oil refining, the prosperity of those islands is in serious jeopardy as of this writing.

So marked was the absence of Sabian men that early travelers dubbed the place the "Island of Women"—a name that seemed to conjure up exotic romance but basically represented a bitter economic truth. In modern times, the men have been inclined to migrate to the larger, richer Dutch islands of Aruba and Curaçao, both of which have giant refinery complexes. The emigrants now often take along their families, however, and even children from families that stay on Saba are often sent away to Aruba or Curaçao for schooling. These factors are breaking down the historic isolation of Saba. By collecting the life histories of a cross section of islanders, the researcher was attempting to describe the traditional island culture before it vanished. The results of that project were presented by Crane (1987).

Some years later, the author initiated a follow-up study. If the earlier life history collection was designed to capture a traditional society on the wane, then it seemed desirable to compare it with a society being created, one also seen "from the inside." Aruba, to which so many Sabians had migrated, was selected. Its Chamber of Commerce boasted that it was home to persons of sixty-six different nationalities, a remarkably polyglot group to have been grafted onto an island that, until the founding of Lago, the great oil refinery (at one time the world's largest), had been virtually a desert island, lacking in large-scale plantation agriculture and far off the main trade routes. And yet Aruba did not resemble a transient labor camp. There were elements of social stability in the cultural matrix the migrants were joining, and the island was conspicuously lacking in crime, grinding poverty, or pollution—all the more surprising given the circumstances of its rapid growth. Moreover, the year in which the research was to be conducted was the fiftieth anniversary of the establishment of Lago, and the Arubians were in a retrospective frame of mind.

Chapter 4 discussed some of the ambiguities inherent in the analysis of collective life histories. The Aruba project illustrates some of these problems quite clearly. In the first place, its model was the study of the rural English village of Akenfield (Blythe 1974). In that study, the researchers had collected the reminiscences of the villagers in traditional life history fashion. The resulting book had chapter headings that reflected the conventional rubrics of "community studies" in anthropology and sociology (for example, "work," "education," "law," "social mores"), but the contents of those chapters were simply the words of the villagers themselves as they addressed these topics. The result seems to be an intimate and affecting portrait of Akenfield as told by its residents.

Akenfield presents a trap for those who would replicate its methods. Most fundamentally, the absence of obvious analysis by the editor yields only an illusion of spontaneity. Given the fact that the text is composed of snippets taken out of larger discourses (whether in or out of context the reader has no way of knowing), it is obvious that, even without interposing his own words, the editor has, in fact, "composed" the book. It is an elaborately arranged symphony, albeit the component melodic phrases were originally the villagers'.

The organizational rubrics clearly reflect the concerns of the social scientist, not the farmers and craftsmen who probably saw their community as a whole, not divided into conventionalized slots. The book's overall gently elegiac tone certainly reflects the attitudes of urban observers of the fading rural lifeways, but does it reflect the villagers' outlook? Might their expressions of nostalgia and regret have been fleeting thoughts embedded in statements of bold confidence in future progress? There simply is no way of knowing.

It was therefore decided that any published results of the Aruba project (e.g., Angrosino 1982) would include clearly labeled statements of analysis. The informants' words would be used to illustrate analytical points, but no claim would be advanced that alternative analytical schemes could not also be supported in the words of the life history texts. Publication of the complete texts (fifty-five were eventually recorded) was impossible, and, because excerpted materials would always be the results of editorial choice, it was deemed best simply to identify them as such.

Whatever the integrity of the completed text may be, a serious general problem inheres in the data. Even if somehow all fifty-five texts were published together, without analysis at all, what would they add up to? It would be fatuous to claim that fifty-five stories by anybody could form a complete record of the historical, social, cultural, and psychological life of an island of more than sixty thousand inhabitants. Given the time-consuming nature of life history elicitation techniques, one may not hope to collect many more more than fifty-five life histories in any one field season. Even if all sixty thousand residents could somehow be interviewed, how could any sense be made out of the resulting mountain of data without exercise of editorial choice?

The fifty-five respondents, then, represent themselves. They are persons who certainly typify prominent segments of Aruba's current resident population, as identified through conventional participant-observational research. As a group, they provide a broad overview of current ways of life on the island. But it must also be admitted that, given the pressures of time, the persons who turned out to be the most cooperative informants were those who were either the most sophisticated (those who understood and approved of the goals of the research project) or the least sophisticated (who went along just out of politeness). In either group, they tended to be persons who were unusually articulate. Because each informant was sent a typed transcript of the interview and was asked to sign a release form indicating permission to quote from it, the resulting texts were the products of persons capable of self-conscious reflection about the image they wanted to project about themselves. All these factors limit the representativeness of the results even further, though they may well heighten their interest as documents of the interaction process itself (an aspect of autobiographical research to which, unfortunately, I did not begin to pay much attention until later).

A third general issue concerns the nature of the documents themselves. Some of them might legitimately be called life histories, but a fair number of them—on the informants' own initiative, I believe—turned out to possess a quite different character. A number of the informants, particularly those who had migrated to Aruba in search of a better life (which, such things being relative, they almost invariably found), brushed aside their early lives and concentrated on how they found their jobs at the refinery or in one of the service trades it spawned and what the resulting material prosperity had meant to them. Even native Arubians who felt inclined to include picturesque anecdotes about the old days were far more interested in the here and now and how their own lives had changed for the better with the advent of the oil boom.

For these reasons, I felt it best to label such stories "personal narratives," as defined in chapter 1, because they cannot be taken as records of people's entire lives. I do not, however, see this more restricted term as a drawback. Indeed, the present and future orientation is the most salient feature of the Arubian narratives, and it is one that, I believe, accurately reflects the evolving culture and value system of a society on the move and impressed with its own relative success and prosperity. To have forced the informants to dwell on their childhoods in order to satisfy some criterion of completeness or out of a misplaced faith in traditional psychoanalytical explanations would have severely distorted the view of themselves and of their society that the Arubians were satisfied to project.

In view of this bias inherent in the informants' own view of their circumstances, it was decided that published accounts of the Arubian materials would eschew the analytical rubrics of the community study (which, as in Akenfield, give the impression of continuity with the traditions of bygone social stability) in favor of headings that reflected a theory of modernization.

One such theory that seems consonant with the personalistic approach is that of Peacock and Kirsch (1970), who point out that modernization is not only a matter of new economic and political institutions but represents a new way of looking at the world. Their model suggests four broad themes (increased rate of change, social differentiation, universalization, and rationalization of personal identity) that characterize the process of modernization, and material from the Aruba personal narratives illustrates it.*

---

* This section is taken, with some modification, from Angrosino 1982:105–15.

Increased Rate of Change

Although it may be taken as axiomatic that all cultures change through time, technological innovation and complexity seem to stimulate relatively rapid change in all aspects of the culture (that is, in beliefs, as well as in activities). It is therefore interesting that the perception of accelerated change is recorded as a topic in a number of the personal narratives under study. It may be obvious that persons caught in a dramatic situation of change will feel that things are changing too fast. But how do persons in such a situation deal with that feeling?

The discussion of rapid change is most frequent in the personal narratives of the Arubian natives. Their stories are often quite explicit in making the contrast between the old days before Lago and now. The contrast usually focuses on the hard times of the old days. This theme is expressed succinctly by one native man, now a computer programmer at Lago. He says of his youth, "Remember that Lago wasn't here at that time and there was nothing for them to do. It was a real bad time."

The stories of the migrants even provide a variant of this theme. A number of them talk about how quiet and peaceful Aruba was when they first came there and the rustic rectitude of its people—all in sharp contrast with things as they seem to be today. However, they are not inclined to discuss the economic hardships associated with that quiet past. A man from the United States, now head of a printing firm, responded to a question on the nature of the people, "The island was a place, at that time that was unbelievable. There were homes then that never closed the doors, much less locked them. . . . There was a friendliness about the people."

The migrants, far more than the natives, are conscious of the seeming breakdown in Arubian family life. As evidence they point to the prevalence of unchaperoned girls out on dates, declining church attendance, the appearance of teenage street-corner idlers, and so forth. What is interesting in these stories is that the migrants seem to have a divided consciousness; they rarely, if ever, discuss such changes in terms of their own lives. It is as if they have long since accepted their marginality with respect to Aruba and their status as transients in its society.

Change can be measured only against some standard of stability. Lacking such a standard in their own lives, the migrants are apt to overemphasize the rooted stability of the Arubian past and hence overestimate the accelerating pace of change in that society. Clearly, the anthropologist might well see the migrants themselves as a symptom of social change rather than as merely interested bystanders to it. But it is equally important to understand that these persons characteristically do not see themselves as involved in the process, other than as observers.

Social Differentiation

In the folk society, considerable overlapping of roles occurs: an individual may be mother's brother, father-in-law, shaman, and war leader all at once. In modern societies, there are more persons with whom individuals relate, but they tend to play one role at a time. This trend toward specialization is referred to in the Peacock and Kirsch model as "social differentiation." Although it is not always the case, such specialization can often lead to a high degree of social mobility, insofar as many specializations are acquired skills that require persons to move in order to be trained or to find employment. When specialized skills are acquired, individuals can be in a position to sell their labor in an open labor market (if one exists), and their economic decisions about relocation need not have very much to do with familial or other traditional loyalties.

This constellation of behaviors is clearly marked in the Arubian narratives. In the stories of the natives, a sharp contrast is evident between the extremely localized, family-centered system of pre-Lago days and the current condition. The most striking aspect of this change, as the natives see it, is not so much their personal acquisition of specialized skills but the fact that they have come to encounter so many different persons. They really take to heart the Chamber of Commerce boast about the island's heterogeneity. They may simply have been guarded or polite in telling their stories, but the complete absence in the natives' narrative of any real animosity toward outsiders and their potentially disruptive ways is striking. The Arubians are supposed to be conservative and clannish, but they have welcomed the newcomers and have reveled in their international contacts. One native put it this way: "In the lab like I was, we had people from all over—from Czechoslovakia [even]—but the official business was done in English, so no matter how you spoke it, we all got along."

A somewhat different picture emerges from the stories of the migrants, for they clearly see an implicit differentiation between foreigners and Arubians. Again, no animosity is expressed, but the migrants generally feel that they have never really been accepted. Green (1976:102) has noted that in Curaçao the natives were willing to accept strangers only so long as they learned the local languages; this has not been the case on Aruba. It is interesting to note that the more recent migrants there are far more sanguine about their assimilation than are those of longer standing. Recent arrivals, and those from the United States generally, are particularly enthusiastic about their ability to "get in with the people," whereas older migrants realize, with a touch of regret, that even after twenty-five years or more, they are still not considered Arubian.

For example, a young widow who had accompanied her artist husband to the island has become the executive assistant to one of the island's leading entrepreneurs. Although she criticizes the "typical American" attitude of many who live and work on the island, she herself expresses an optimistic American approach to the question of assimilation:

> My approach to living in a foreign place is not typically American because I find it rather a waste of time to insulate yourself in a colony or in an area like the strip along the beach here in Aruba. In doing that, you do not reap the benefits of getting to know another culture or another ethnic group.... Actually, all you have to do is to be receptive. You don't have your mind closed, because it's a lot more fun to be receptive.

An older man who came to Aruba to work at Lago and went

on to found his own insurance company has become something of a local institution; in fact, he and his wife feel "right at home." After a discussion of the current political scene, he stopped and mused, "I said 'we' there, so I suppose I identify myself with Aruba now. I identify myself with the refinery also, because that's the lifeblood of the island. I often say, 'We export 500,000 barrels a day,' although I'm not at all a part of Lago."

On the other hand, a young black man from St. Thomas grew up feeling Arubian, and yet, "Really, to be in a puzzle all your life is no good, reared up in confusion. . . . They don't do it any more, discriminate, you know. But before they used to do it. They considered themselves, you know, the native Arubians, to be really pure. Any strangers? Nah!"

A Guyanese woman, an Aruba resident since the late 1940s, adds, "No matter how long you've lived [here] . . . you never really seem to get to know the people well, you never get the feeling of belonging. They always make it so pointing that 'you're not one of us'—in an indirect way, of course, but you can feel it."

The West Indian foreigners were often seen by the Arubians to be just as clannish as the latter were viewed by outsiders. The Surinamers were thought to be especially standoffish. One of this group, a resident in Aruba since World War II, says, "We Surinamers had the Club Surinam in San Nicolaas, which is still here and pretty active again today. In that place, all the Surinamers used to get together because you could buy all the Surinam dishes that we all liked very much." This same individual, however, has been one of the island's (and Lago's) most outstanding success stories. He has worked his way through the Lago ranks to head the company's maintenance department. He was the first locally hired employee (that is, not European or North American) to be permitted to build a home in the once exclusive enclave of Seroe Colorado (known as "The Colony"). His position as head of the maintenance department puts him in direct charge of the day-to-day activities of Seroe Colorado, and this makes him, he jokes, "like the mayor of this town." Perhaps because of his close association with the elite expatriate commu-

nity and its ideas and activities, he has not become very much of
an Arubian. "I don't consider myself as much an Arubian as I
would have had I more contact with them." he states.

A variant on this theme is expressed by a Trinidadian migrant
who points out, "I have always considered this Aruba a place of
temporary sojourn, or [as] if it was that I'm leaving tomorrow.
We are here only as birds of passage, but this has gone on for
twenty-odd years." He attempts to maintain his ties to his
"home," but, "When I go back [maybe every six years or so],
and ask, 'Is this the Trinidad I knew?' I must say, 'No.' My
friends don't even know me. And so back I come to Aruba."

A similar sentiment is expressed by a Guyanese migrant who
had once been involved in the health professions and is now in
private business. He says, "I came to Aruba with the intention of
staying here just four years, saving some money and then getting
out to [study medicine]. But it turns out that I am still here. Now
the hospitality that I've gotten in Aruba—well, I'm not the best
friend of everybody, not everybody has been nice to me. And
that makes me think that life is where you make it."

An even stronger statement along those lines is that of an
elderly Jewish merchant who says:

> I consider myself an Arubian now and I hope they accept me too.
> Normally they say I'm "one of the good ones." . . . To be honest,
> when I first came here, I was so young and so scared that I didn't
> know what I was doing—I almost didn't know where I was. The
> only plan I had was to make a living. I had practically no money.
> My first money that I left from home with—some thirty-odd
> dollars—I lost at the boat. But this has been a good life for me
> here in Aruba ever since. I belong here and when people make a
> party I'll be invited. As a matter of fact, two of my boys were
> bar mitzvahed here. . . . We have . . . only eighteen Jewish
> families, but I had over six hundred people at those things—with
> a priest included!

These examples provide two rather different perceptions of
the same social process, although both groups clearly recognize

the differentiating, specializing tendency to which they both respond. What is most intriguing, however, is that it is the migrants who are most impressed by the in-group/out-group dichotomy of Arubian society, and the natives themselves seem to feel that they are making great strides in internationalizing themselves and breaking down traditional communal barriers. The apparent communalism of the society is diluted by a realization of a growing interdependency of specialized roles; this may be one reason for the relative harmony (to date) within the Arubian melting pot.

Universalization

By universalization, Peacock and Kirsch mean the trend toward social organization based on achievement rather than ascription. It is by far the most significant theme of the personal narratives, particularly those of the native Arubians. It is also the only component of the modernization process about which they express some real regret. Traditional Aruba was a strongly kin-based society in which relatives of both one's father and one's mother lived in the same district; this large group of kin all interacted frequently with one another. This relationship is spoken of with extreme warmth and affection almost invariably, and even foreigners, when asked to comment on their first impressions of Aruba, tend to talk about how impressed they were with the closeness of family life. An image of the old pattern is provided by a woman from one of the island's leading old families:

> Our home was built in pieces. The center piece belonged to my great-grandparents. The old Arubian way of starting a house is with a center room, with the possibility of building on both sides. In 1907, my grandmother and my aunt built onto the side because my parents were then living in the center piece. Later on when my brothers and sisters were coming back from boarding school and the house was getting too small—because in the meantime we had the smaller ones, the babies, being added to the family—they added a third piece.

Nowadays, the natives admit that the old family ties are in decline, although they are far from dead. For example, one middle-aged man says, "My wife is my second cousin. Of course, now people have other things to do, so they don't get married—but in those days there was nothing to do but get married."

Foreigners also seem keenly aware of this decline and point to it as the root cause of what they perceive to be the island's future trouble as a "mixed-up society." Nevertheless, it should be noted that the close-knit traditional family situation was always very definitely undercut by a sense of personal pride, which seems to fit in very well with the modern emphasis on personal ambition. As an older gentleman, a retired Lago technician, put it, "On the average, I would guess that people in those days married when they were twenty-three, twenty-four years old; I got married younger, but that was because I could afford it then because I had a job at Lago—and I wanted to get married."

The industrial system did not, over the long run, disrupt the pattern of residence and family ties, which is one of the key reasons why the advent of Lago did not lead to the creation of workers' slums or other manifestations of social disintegration, at least among the native population. (A slum area known as "The Village" has, in fact, grown up near the refinery, but its residents have always been predominantly transient foreigners.) One parish priest explains: "One thing that doesn't change, though, is the family pride. When you say, for example, the family Tromp, I can tell you they come from Noord. When you say family Dijkhof, they live in Paradera. When you say Schwengle, de Kort, de Cuba, it's Savaneta; Geerman, it's Santa Cruz. Each family has its own residential area, and that keeps them together." But, on the other hand, "people here feel that 'this is our parish.' It is really something of that, with the consequence, also, that they don't accept so easily people from outside."

Nevertheless, Lago had a more subtle but perhaps more pervasive effect in its enshrinement of a merit system that made industrial skills and ambitions of individuals paramount over family connections. One migrant describes the changes in the Arubian character generated by Lago:

> People's attitudes toward work has gotten much more responsible. Long ago a man worked Monday, Tuesday, Wednesday, Thursday, and Friday, and he would have halfday on Saturday to get drunk all through the rest of the weekend. So it ended up he really didn't work Monday because he was in no shape to work. Now that has changed; people work and they take consideration and care of themselves to get back on the job. Of course, they've paid a big price, because many of them were discharged, lost benefits, and things like that. So that taught them the lesson of a more responsible life.

Although it is still true that people inherit jobs at the refinery from relatives, this method is not now, and never has been, the dominant mode of job placement. It remains a minor but noticeable factor in obtaining government jobs as well. Because jobs at the refinery really do provide security, they have come to dominate other economic activities such as farming, and hence their particular style of universalized relationships has come to the fore.

Even a man who recognizes the value of having job skills comparable to those of a refinery worker in Kuwait or Texas such that he has become an interchangeable cog in an international system will express regret at the loss of the sturdy values of home and kin. The Chilean-born director of the YMCA, in fact, discusses at some length the difference between the family-oriented Arubians and the "West Indians," by which he means the people from the British Caribbean islands living in The Village. The latter are "afflicted" with disrupted families; and, moreover, he sees his own role as being a kind of surrogate father to the children of that community whose fathers are absent. In so saying, he echoes the fear among the Arubians that their own family relationships may someday be similarly disrupted.

Even some of the younger informants express fear that the remaining family system will not survive, and they see this as a negative factor in an otherwise exciting and challenging future. The head of the island's social work department, in fact, cites the British social anthropologist Elizabeth Bott and explicitly characterizes Aruba as an emerging loose-knit network: "Arubian families are leaving that structure of the extended family, and each family is moving toward the nuclear family idea. That's why we have a lot of problems because [of finances]—the family [used to be able to] help each other. That's falling off. We have a problem with the aged . . . that wasn't a problem ever [before]." He goes on to point out that divorce, once considered something only foreigners did, is now frequent among younger Arubians. Nowadays, he says, the community as a whole is tolerant of divorced persons, an unthinkable attitude a generation ago.

But the continuing centrality of family is illustrated by the story of a middle-aged Arubian man, currently a high-ranking airline executive and formerly a recording and television star. Despite his long career as a man of the world, he still allows, "Now the greatest happiness we have is our grandson. He is eighteen months. You can't imagine how happy we are when he comes here. . . . I've traveled a lot, of course, but now I want to remain here in Aruba with my little family." Once a well-regarded composer of love songs, he now proudly plays his favorite recent tune, "A Baby's Smile."

A young woman from a traditional family in the countryside demonstrates her break with tradition by articulating a desire to pursue a career as an artist, yet she stresses family loyalty in her story. She begins by saying, "I am very proud of my family" and ends by stating, "I like to visit other places, but it is not like Aruba, which is something very special to me."

A different kind of universalization is represented by a woman from the United States whose comments on her personal situation in Aruba are interesting because of her emphasis on the differences her expatriation have meant to her as a woman, rather than as an American specifically. She explains, "It's the difference made by going to work. . . . It took away a lot of the rough edges, the uphill fighting that you often have to do in that situation [being left a widow]. I think—no, I'm sure that it was a big plus for me, one which I would not have found in the States."

Rationalization of Personal Identity

In a traditional society, one saw oneself as a member of a group; in a modern society, the individual is a separable unit. Modern society is predicated, moreover, on the individual's ability to plan his or her life. This goal-oriented outlook, so different from the supposed "timelessness" of traditional society, is what Peacock and Kirsch call "rationality." This theme is best seen in the form of the narratives, even more than in their content. The Aruba informants tended to tell chronological stories, often with a rags-to-riches theme, in some contrast to those of the Saba informants.

The most striking such success story is that of the YMCA director, who ends his chronicle, "You know, God helped me out on the way, and I'm here now to help others do the same." His story seems like a real-life analog of a Horatio Alger tale, featuring a poor but honest youngster, a rich benefactor, and how the boy grew up to repay that benefactor and carry on his ideals of public service. Unlike informants in more traditional societies who are loath to admit to success for fear of provoking jealousy, the Arubians are very pleased to have achieved it, and they expressed few reservations about telling the world how they did.

The social work department head, however, made a point of noting that native Arubians participate in an "avoidance culture": "Nobody wants to stand in the spotlight. They want to stay . . . as anonymous as possible." Hence, the Arubian rationalization of the life arc does not take the form of strong individualism. Rather, there is a kind of missionizing tendency, a desire to bring everyone up to one's own level, to create a crowd of people all moving along in the same direction so that one need not stand out. Hence, despite the supposed isolation and conservatism of traditional Arubian society, a spirit of bandwagoning makes for a maintenance of solidarity even as the material aspects of the society are changing.

Migrants of the lower classes came to Aruba simply to obtain decent jobs, and, like migrants elsewhere in the Third World, they had no particular career goals. But, among those who came with professional or technical skills, the island is seen quite explicitly as a place to work out a rational life plan, and even retirees devote much energy to planning how to keep up with things. It should be noted, however, that women are not encouraged to plan their lives in this way; for them, being wives and mothers is still supposed to be sufficient. One female social worker had recently returned from representing the Dutch islands at an international women's conference. She pointed out that single women especially had a terrible time getting jobs at all and that those who work for the government are still supposed to be dismissed immediately upon marriage because women with husbands to support them can continue to work only at the risk of disgracing their families.

The Arubian narratives reveal a society in transition. People still express concern over the apparent disregard for traditional values, and they express a nostalgia for the ordered, integrated world of their past. And yet, the opinion leaders of the society are just as actively engaged in bringing ways of thinking in line with social changes that have already occurred. Because the society is now built out of persons of diverse backgrounds, this process is quite different from one taking place in a society in which a homogeneous, dominant community acts as a conservative force against imported change.

Through Lago, Aruba is part of the international oil system; there is no way that its residents can feel that their "little island in the sun" is "just a dot on the map," common expressions elsewhere in the Caribbean. The people are well aware that events in Saudi Arabia or Japan or the United States or Venezuela have immediate impact on their day-to-day lives. They are proud of the island's new multilingual capabilities, which serve to link it to a new system of beliefs and actions.

The old social system of local interests and kin interdependencies is being replaced by an international political-economic system, and the old cultural system of valued localized loyalties and the influence of folk Catholicism is in the process of being replaced by one in which political and economic power are centralized in distant metropoles, whose values and ways of life are, perforce, desirable. These conflicting values are clearly demonstrated in the words of the people themselves. Despite the manifest limitations of data such as these, they can still be used to glimpse the multifarious reality of a changing society as it is experienced by those living therein. An analytical scheme is necessary because the facts cannot and do not speak for themselves; such a scheme should be chosen to reflect the internally perceived force of change rather than the social researcher's preconceptions about the nature of the community.

6 /
Life Histories of Deinstitutionalized Retarded Adults: An Interactionist Approach

THE PRECEDING CHAPTERS have dealt with three research investigations, each of which made use of some variant of the life history method. Both the advantages and the limitations of using autobiographical data in such social research have been discussed. These three projects reflect the standard view of the life history method as a text-centered approach in that autobiographies were believed to be useful to the extent that they contained factual information (or impressionistic material that can be interpreted as if it were factual) about individual personalities or the nature of societies, cultures, or historical periods.

The alternative view, that the essence of autobiography is in the interactive process of its creation, did not play a part in my approach until I developed a more recent project. By its nature, this research has called into question in a direct way many of the conventional assumptions about autobiographical data in the social science context.

Since 1981 I have been conducting studies of deinstitutionalization policy in Tennessee, Florida, and Washington, DC (Angrosino 1981; Angrosino 1985; Angrosino and Whiteford 1986). I have worked most intensively with adults released from institutional custody into community-based treatment agencies in the Tampa Bay area of Florida and have centered my activities in a program that I have referred to in public presentations as Opportunity House (OH). OH was the first community-based agency in Florida to deal with clients whose primary diagnosis is mental retardation but who also have psychiatric problems. Moreover, the clients have all been in trouble with the law, and most have been adjudicated to OH in lieu of prison.

"Handicapping" or "disabling" conditions are, by definition, culture-bound concepts. One is handicapped only to the degree that one cannot "fulfill certain valued social roles," in Parsons's classic phrase (Parsons 1972:107); and those roles are determined, as we would probably all agree, by the norms of the social setting. In our society, physical prowess is less valuable in the job market than intellectual capacity. Because one's ability to be "productive" is a paramount marker of social identity in our culture, people with intellectual deficits are truly handicapped. Retarded people are "trained" largely because in our society it is unconscionable for an otherwise able-bodied person to do nothing productive, but the retarded are trained for jobs that our culture defines as not really worth doing. To lack the intellectual capacity for the most valued social roles is seen as outside the mainstream of culture; from that position, the attribution of a less-than-human status is not far off.

Retardation means that victims are slowed in their ability to learn (Haywood 1970). *Slow* does not mean never, and yet the word has taken on that connotation in popular, pejorative speech. The label *retarded* has indeed become a stigma. And yet, of the estimated 5 to 6 million persons so labeled in the United States, fewer than 20 percent fall into the categories of severely or profoundly retarded, in which learning capacity is so restricted as to be negligible (Edgerton 1979). The rest of that large population, most of whom are now deinstitutionalized, have learning capacities that are literally slowed down but by no means absent. But since they are incapable of fulfilling the most valued roles in our society, they may as well be the helpless nonpersons of popular myth.

Retarded persons have not often figured in the studies of social scientists, perhaps because they have not been seen as meaningful bearers of culture. The main exception has been the work of the anthropologist Robert Edgerton, who was working on a cross-cultural definition of incompetence as early as the 1960s (Edgerton 1970) and whose classic study *The Cloak of Competence* (1967) still stands as the paradigmatic ethnography of deinstitutionalized mentally retarded people. His multidisciplinary research team at UCLA has produced volumes of working papers on the social ecology of these individuals over the past decade. The sociologist Daryl Evans, working in the Edgerton tradition of qualitative methodology, has also produced a noteworthy ethnographic account of the experiences of retarded adults (Evans 1983).

These studies collectively stress the concept of adaptation in a way that roughly parallels recent studies of the community organization of other disadvantaged minorities. The trend is away from viewing the life ways of these people as degenerated approximations of middle-class mainstream norms and toward seeing these people as capable of building up alternative community networks that enable them to cope with, and perhaps even confront or surmount, the demands of that mainstream.

Some evidence suggests that retarded people, contrary to the stereotypes, are amenable to conventional survey research techniques, provided the researchers come equipped with "patience and well constructed questions, without forced categories and without ambiguous or complex phrasing" (Wyngaarden 1981: 113). The majority opinion, however, is that of Sigelman et al. (1981), who review a variety of studies and conclude that the results are "discouraging." Even in the most carefully designed studies, a consistent bias seems to exist in the form of "acquiescence": retarded people seem to know what the interviewer is after and, socialized into ready compliance, give the answers that seem called for rather than the ones they truly feel. This finding, incidentally, is suggestive of the adaptive learning capacities of retarded people, but it does not bode well for the utility of a questionnaire methodology. Indeed, Bercovici (1981), speaking for the UCLA group, has issued a call for participant-observation ethnographic methods as the only suitable way to work with retarded people in community settings. Of the specific data collection techniques associated with this general orientation, none has been more promising than that of the life history.

The retardation literature contains considerable biographical material, mostly in the form of caretakers' accounts of their experiences with retarded family members. On occasion, these accounts include brief, pointillistic narratives by the retarded persons themselves, on the assumption that "the life of a retarded man or woman is as simple as a 'little song' . . . or, on the other hand, a complex spiritual burden to be borne by only the most dedicated of parents" (Whittemore, Koegel, and Langness 1980:2).

Among the few attempts at presenting autobiography are those by Hunt (1967), Seagoe (1964), and McCune (1973), all of them in a kind of popular-inspirational genre rather than in the scientific tradition. Nevertheless, the common theme of these three life stories is opportunity. The central figures do not see themselves as a "helpless victims" or as the shell of "the person who might have been," but rather as people who learn what their limitations are and go on from there. Could more thorough methods of elicitation pick up on this theme and thereby help overcome the stereotypes of the retarded adult as one devoid of identity and a nonparticipant in culture except as a passive reactor to the stimuli of caretakers?

The UCLA group has collected life histories extensively over the past two decades, gaining experience that has recently been published in an anthology (Langness and Levine 1986). Some obvious technical problems exist, however, in working with retarded informants. For one thing, linguistic research has demonstrated that they characteristically make few "first mentions" in their narratives. That is, they tend to plunge into their story, not bothering to establish that the listener knows anything about the people, places, or events being referred to (Kernan and Sabsay 1985:4).

Retarded persons also typically exhibit a variety of deficits in language production, including restricted vocabulary, syntax below age expectations, relatively shorter sentences, relatively less abstraction, and frequent sacrifice of conventional meaning in favor of inner, private, individual meaning (Linder 1978:1). These deficits, however, have been recorded mostly in clinical settings where retarded persons, like disadvantaged persons in general, tend to be reticent.

In fact, a closer analysis of those same clinical data demonstrates that retarded persons can manage their deficits in quiet but efficient ways. They have, for example, a sense of timing in narrative structure, revealing crucial information after building carefully to a climax. They also know how to vary their response to the same question, depending on the setting—the more clinical the setting, the more correct or deferential the answer (Linder 1978:13–15). Linder suspects that retarded speech is not so much "flawed" as it is "stigmatized." Clinicians expect it to be deficient, so they hear deficiencies, ignoring the adaptive capabilities in the use of speech as a medium of communication beneath the surface errors of grammar or word usage.

Kernan and Sabsay (1985:1) point out that studies of the language competence of retarded subjects have focused on sentence-construction capabilities. These form only a small part of overall communicative competence, which also includes recognizing the linguistic rules and conventions that apply to conversation in a given community. Retarded speakers do, in fact, exhibit deficiencies in this regard, but their major problems involve the organizing of thoughts—relating, for example, the ideas of one sentence in a logical fashion to those in the next. This problem is not, of course, restricted to retarded people. For the rest, retarded speakers' sentences may be "grammatically ill formed" but usually are not unintelligible. Lexical selection may be idiosyncratic, but again not to the point of indecipherability (unless the subject is also psychotic). In longer narratives, retarded people tend to make numerous false starts— introductions of thoughts that are quickly abandoned. Like the other errors, this fault can also be found in the speech of nonretarded subjects, although retarded persons may exhibit it with greater frequency or may exhibit all these faults at the same time (Kernan and Sabsay 1985:35).

A longer narrative, such as one collected from one of the author's own informants, is generally said to consist of an abstract ("I'm going to tell you about when I was a kid"), an orientation ("We used to live in Miami when I was a little kid"), some complicating action ("But then my mom and dad split up and we had to move to my grandma's"), an evaluation ("I didn't like my grandma—she hit me a lot"), a resolution ("So I was always running away until I got sent to Opportunity House"), and a coda ("And that's where I been living since I was eighteen"). Retarded people sometimes scramble their logical narrative sequence, but they rarely omit key elements. In comparison with the narratives of speakers of normal intelligence, they overstress the evaluation section, dwelling on interior feelings more than on orienting details. One of my informants, in telling about a foster home where he used to live, kept repeating how bad it was, how he was always getting hurt. He spoke with such vehemence and concentration that I assumed at first that his foster parents beat him regularly. It turned out that the parents were very nice, but they had a large boxer dog that used to run up to him and knock him down.

In addition to problems related to linguistic production, the life history approach is problematic when used with retarded subjects because of their short attention spans. There might also be a problem in that the lives of these people have often been so unhappy that they are reluctant to retell sad events, and the researcher is reluctant to coax them to do so.

Despite these technical problems, the collection of life histories is still a promising method of finding out about the interior lives of people heretofore believed not to have any. As Edgerton (1984:2) explains:

> It is the consensus of [the] literature [about deinstitutionalized mentally retarded persons] that if we are to improve our understanding of the community adaptation of retarded persons, we must study their lives holistically, where they occur rather than in laboratories, and we must listen to these persons as they express their own views of their lives.

My OH informants are not typical of retarded adults in general. If, however, a data-collection technique can be used successfully with subjects having so many confounding barriers to easy communication, then that technique may be said to have indicated its value.

To date, I have collected life history materials from twenty of the OH clients—all men, ranging in age from twenty-two to forty-four years. Of these, ten may be said to be essentially completed records as far as the objective details of life events may be concerned. These numbers reflect, to some degree, the fact that the life history collection has been a personal effort squeezed into a larger, cooperative research effort that has had other aims. They also, more importantly, reflect the slow pace of collection that is caused by barriers discussed above. Another factor contributing to delay has been the equipment used. My informants seem comfortable with my use of a tape recorder, and so I have taped all the interviews. Because many of the individuals have some speech impediments, it has been difficult to find people who are both sufficiently skilled at transcribing from tape and able to understand the subjects' speech. I have therefore had to do much of the transcription myself, a time-consuming task. At any rate, because of the small number of cases, I must disavow any claims to representativeness of my informant population, although I believe that the qualitative data generated by the interviews at least suggest of further research directions.

In my research I have encountered most of the technical barriers discussed in the literature. My most serious problem, however, was not that my informants had a short attention span and wandered off the subject but rather that they were so flattered that someone actually seemed interested in them as persons that they attacked the task with tenacity. Most of them exhausted my limited allotted time—and, in some cases, my patience—long before I exhausted theirs. I had minimal difficulty with substandard linguistic production; my informants' discourses are not elegantly shaped, but they are not gibberish. On the literary level, their simple directness is sometimes surprisingly affecting.

In collecting life histories from informants of normal intelligence, I have tried to be as nondirective as possible and have not insisted on any particular order of topics or themes to be dealt with. In my work with retarded subjects, I began by being very directive indeed. With my first few informants, in fact, I found myself virtually walking them through a year-by-year account of their lives and using numerous prompts ("And what happened next?" "And how did you feel about that?") at the slightest pause. This overbearing style of interviewing was not congenial to me, and it gradually became clear that it was not even necessary. As word of my interests spread among the clients at OH, there was some excitement about who would be chosen next. By the time the turn of some of the most eager clients came around, they knew so thoroughly from their friends what I was after that they brushed aside my prompts with knowing smiles. One subject liked to pepper his story with dramatic pauses; the first time he did so, he was obviously expecting me to jump in, so he put his hand over the tape recorder and whispered, "It's OK, I know what I'm doing." He repeated this caution whenever he felt he needed to depart from a strictly chronological narrative in order to make a point. Although this individual is exceptionally "high functioning" and had a keen grasp of how he wanted to put his story together, his confidence loosened me up as well, and I became progressively more willing to allow other, less clever informants to tell their stories in their own way, in their own good time. More recently, I have tried to go back to some of the first informants and let them retell their stories, if they wanted to do so, without my coercive instructions. In these cases, I found little variation in objective data but much richer elaboration of feelings, attitudes, and opinions—the subjects not only expressed emotions but tried to explain why they felt as they did.

This change may also have been due to a greater familiarity with me as an interviewer. At the beginning, I now suspect, I was probably regarded with some suspicion. Although not a doctor, psychologist, social worker, or house parent, I was still clearly an outsider with some sort of prestige and so was treated with deference. As in many cases where informants perceive a status gap between themselves and a researcher, responses tended to be politely evasive and emotively noncommital. I suspect, too, that some of the early informants thought I could be used to help them "score points" with the authorities, so I was the recipient of a fair amount of manipulative soft-soaping.

However, I have engaged in a modified version of participant observation at OH for five years, and although many of the clients still do not know exactly what I'm doing, I have become a familiar figure. Some have chosen to treat me as a confidant or a go-between to staff; others have sought me out for advice on everything from how to set a wristwatch to how to ask a girl for a date. Even those who do not think of me as a friend in those terms, though, at least have come to the conclusion that I'm harmless, which, given the lives they have led, is a bigger achievement that it may sound. As a result, the interviews have grown more richly, openly subjective through natural processes and probably would have done so even without the conscious change in elicitation technique.

Although I was still unsure of my approach, I worked closely with the staff psychologist to select informants who were reasonably emotionally stable as well as reasonably articulate. Such stability is often only a brittle facade. One young man seemed very cool and self-confident; he began the interview by insisting that, unlike the "other bozos," he'd had a happy life. He blithely shrugged off the circumstances that led him to jail as "just kid stuff," but his mood darkened when he talked about the few days he was forced to spend in jail before his sentence was suspended and he was sent to OH. He blurted out that he had been raped by his cell mate. He cried bitterly and demanded to know whether God would still punish him even though it wasn't his fault.

It was one of those moments all fieldworkers must surely have when they decide that they'd be happier doing library research exclusively from now on. But, although I ended the interview for that day, I didn't abandon my informant, and we spent a long time talking through his problem with the recorder turned off. I am no therapist and avoided giving him "guidance." I simply tried to present a reassuring presence by admitting in all honesty that I was nervous and didn't have all the answers to his problems but that I wanted him to know that I'd be willing to listen to anything he wanted to say. He sobbed and ranted at length, pacing the room in agitation, but kept coming back to take my hand for reassurance.

Afterward, the psychologist marveled at my foolishness, chuckling that the last time a staff member had brought up this topic with the client, the latter had tried to strangle him. Suppressing a desire to strangle the psychologist, I decided that there would be no further point in trying to play it safe. All of us have the capacity for exploding if the wrong nerve is touched, and I would never really learn much about what life is like for these people if I personally kept myself aloof from the possibility that I might see the uglier side of their world and of their own personalities.

As it happens, OH works on a behavior-modification system, and all activities must fit into an individually designed treatment program. Being interviewed by me was defined by staff as an extracurricular activity for which the clients had to earn token points by acceptable behavior. My ability to choose the informants I wanted was therefore limited by the system, so I gradually learned to take whoever was available.

In following a generally interactionist line of analysis, it might be said that whenever people enter the presence of others (that is, any social situation), they are faced with a problem of information control. They cannot reveal everythying, for some important part of their selves must be, in a sense, their most cherished secret. To reveal everything is to become hollow and to lose control of oneself. Persons who fall outside the range of the normal (whether in appearance or behavior) obviously have more to hide than anyone else. Yet their handicap means that the audience has greater power over them than it does over individuals who are more acceptable. People who are stigmatized therefore are in the difficult position of having to surrender more and more of themselves to others in a better position to control the drama and yet of being forced to deny that which makes them special because it is the very thing that forces them into the controlling grasp of others.

Stigmatized people cannot avoid conceptualizing their selfhood in terms of the stigma by which they are labeled by their audience. At the same time, that stigmatization makes them unfit to be part of the audience for others. They are perceived to have no control, so normal people do not need to engage in role playing with them. As a result, a crucial element in the process of identity formation is blocked. In Erving Goffman's theatrical terminology, they are like actors who are the subjects of constant criticism but who are never accorded the opportunity to contribute to the setting of the rules by which the drama is criticized.

Goffman's position can be interpreted to mean that the only source of identification left open to stigmatized people is their sense of shared guilt (Bock 1980:200). They are usually conditioned to feel that in some way they deserve their stigma. My female retarded informants, for example, frequently mention that they were the products of difficult pregnancies and that they "turned out wrong" in punishment for the pain they caused their mothers. They tend to think of others like themselves, therefore, as bad people. Everybody likes to associate with one's own kind, but not when such persons are considered to be bad.

My informants, for example, often prefer to have children as friends because they feel comfortable with companions who aren't too intellectually demanding. Of course, such associations have often gotten them into trouble, when their attentions are misinterpreted as evidence of proclivities toward child molestation. The potential source of support that is to be found in the in-group is thus denied to retarded persons. They will probably never organize themselves on a principle analogous to "Black is beautiful"—the old stigma turned into a new source of pride. On the evidence of my informants' discourses, "dumb" is not thought of as beautiful—the popular/inspirational literature extolling the childlike innocence of the retarded notwithstanding. As one client put it, "I'd rather have all my hands and legs cut off and have to stay in a wheelchair. It'd be better than being a dummy the rest of my life."

According to Goffman, individuals must first be aware of society's disdain in order for them to feel the sting of stigmatization. My evidence suggests that retarded persons are aware of the criticism of their "audience," although probably that audience would prefer to believe that the retarded don't notice or don't care what others think of them. Zetlin and Turner (1984) note that the retarded use a variety of tactics to preserve some sense of self-respect in the face of this one-sided criticism, tactics illustrated by my informants' discourses:

1. *Denial.*—"I ain't dumb like they all think. I could do this reading and stuff if I really wanted to, but I ain't gonna play their game no more."

2. *Passing.*—"You know, if you're like waiting for a bus or something and you can't tell time, all you gotta do is ask somebody, 'Hey, man I forgot to wear my watch today—what time you got?' and they'll give you an answer and never think nothing of it. Even normal people can forget to wear their watch, no? Or like when I go to a restaurant, I always go to MacDonald's, cause I always know what they got to eat and I never got to worry about reading a menu or nothing like that."

3. *Blame attribution.*—"I used to be real smart like all the other kids, you know, but then that f___ing stepfather of mine slapped me around so hard one day he knocked all my brains out."

4. *Tactical dependency.*—"I don't got to worry no more because Mr. Hillson [the instructor at the sheltered workshop] says if I ever get hung up, just give him a call and he'll come take care of me."*

The data are inconclusive on whether the need to engage in these forms of compensation decreases the longer the individual lives outside the institution. The decisive variable in my informant group (a finding shared by Zetlin and Turner) seems to be the attitude of parents. The way in which they (or other significant adult role models) dealt with the retarded child seems to shape not only whether that child will grow up needing to adopt one of these defensive strategies but also which of the defensive tactics will be chosen. Most important, parental attitudes seem to

---

* There is a general concurrence between these interactive strategies and Hankiss's typology of autobiographies that was discussed in chapter two. For example, a case could be made that the denial strategy is associated with a dynastic form of life history. Similarly, passing results in an antithetical style, blame attribution in a self-absolutory strategy, and tactical dependency in a compensatory autobiography.

determine how children will evaluate themselves and their coping strategy as they grow up. The clearest statement to that effect is made by an informant who reflected, "My old man, he always said I was a wimp cause I couldn't fight back—well, I couldn't fight back, you know, cause I was always punier than all the other guys, but the old man, he didn't care. Said I was a wimp and I'd always be a wimp, and I guess he's right. I'm too scared to do—oh, I don't know, to do anything!—without somebody tells me how to do it. I'm always so scared I'll screw it up so I wait till somebody shows me how. I guess the old man was right."

Zetlin and Turner propose four categories into which a retarded subject may be classified with regard to developing a sense of self: (1) acceptors (those who admit to their handicap and who usually adopt a strategy of tactical dependency to get by), (2) qualifiers (those who admit to their handicap but resist thinking of it as irreversible and struggle against their strong feelings that they have done something wrong, usually adopting a blame attribution strategy); (3) vacillators (those who "play retarded" when it suits their purposes but who overall prefer to "pass" if they can); and (4) deniers.

Zetlin and Turner report that their data suggest that acceptors and deniers are older people who have had more experience with the community and the service system (1984:116) and that qualifiers and vacillators are younger people who probably never underwent "total institutionalization" as children and hence are ambivalent both about themselves as well as the community and its support networks. My informant group is probably too small and biased to make comparisons worthwhile, but provisionally I would have to say that this conclusion is not supported by my data, where the strategies and self-perceptions cross-cut age categories.

Ethnicity, not mentioned by Zetlin and Turner, does, however, play a role: blacks tend to be either vacillators or deniers, whites acceptors or qualifiers. I might speculate that black retarded men are not unaware of more general social pressures in the black community, and are unwilling to play a helpless social role and fall back on a handicap as an excuse to be "less than a man." The black men in my group are far more willing—and able—than are the whites to experiment with solving their own problems.

One final interesting conclusion by Zetlin and Turner bears noting: their long-term data suggest that these categories of self-perception tend to remain stable and are not affected even by major changes in life circumstances, such as marriage. In their group, acceptors often end up marrying "normal" (or, at least, more nearly functional) partners and go right on being cared for. I can see some inklings of this pattern in the stories of my older informants (though their psychiatric problems may be getting in the way of their adjustment strategies), but I would need to follow some of the younger ones for a few more years before I could be confident that the pattern occurred more generally.

This preliminary analysis demonstrates some of the possibilities of the interactionist framework for analysis of life history materials. But it is an analysis that once again looks to the text as a "factual" document. Although the analyst in this case is looking for facts about interaction strategies in the lives of retarded informants rather than about early childhood traumas or events of cultural-historical significance, that analyst is still mining the text as if it were a finished product that somehow conveyed all there was to know about an informant's interactive strategies.

When working with autobiographical materials provided by others, there is no choice but to utilize the text as presented. But when collecting the life history in person, are researchers justified in ignoring "the other" to whom the discourse is addressed? Shouldn't researchers treat themselves as integral to the "ethnographic present," as critical components of the development of the personality and character of the informant?

When clients like deinstitutionalized retarded adults are involved, these questions become all the more crucial. Such persons are in many ways members of an exotic culture. It is possible for researchers to sympathize, but scarcely to empathize, with the lives they lead. Even to imagine how they feel is an abstract

intellectual feat that is itself a transcendence of their own thinking capacities. But, unlike the peoples traditionally studied by
anthropologists or recorded by oral historians, retarded persons
do not have the security of their own culture. The "native" informant may cooperate with, even humor, the researcher but does
not have an ultimate stake in the outcome of the interview. If the
interview goes sour, it is the researcher's loss, not the informant's; and, though the latter may feel sorry for having disap-
pointed a guest, he or she knows that that guest is an alien visitor
whose failure does not compromise the informant's own way of
life.

But retarded people are exotics as defined by a social
mainstream; their culture is not a secure haven of retreat but a
place of exile. All of them, particularly those who have been deinstitutionalized, are told throughout their lives that their own
way of doing things is wrong and will get them into trouble, that
only the standards of the mainstream are valuable. Hence, they
are just about the only informants whose stake in the successful
outcome of an interview is as great as the researcher's. A successful interview is a symbolic confirmation of their ability to
function in ways that elicit approval from a representative of the
mainstream. The researcher is therefore not a neutral hand press-
ing the tape-recorder button but a vital accomplice in the
transformation of a despised "retard" into a socially acceptable
person.

At some profound level, there may be a bedrock "culture of
the retarded," a private and satisfying world closed to clinicians
by the inadequacy of current research techniques. But even if
such a culture exists, it is less important to society than the fact
that our larger culture demands that retarded people conform to
the mainstream. For good or ill, the operative culture of the retarded is only the accommodation that they reach with the
mainstream.*

_____

* Detailed ethnographies conducted in societies with a less coercive orientation than ours, and which therefore permit retarded people more latitude in "living
in their own world," would provide important comparative data, but such studies
are almost entirely lacking in the literature at this point.

Under these circumstances, the life history interview cannot be simply a technique designed to elicit objective information as a finished product. The interview is itself the fact, the information, the most relevant source of data. If the culture of the retarded evolves in interactions with the mainstream, and if the interview is a microcosm of those encounters, then the dynamics of the interview become paradigmatic of the emergence of that culture. The same point probably applies readily to studies of handicapped or otherwise deviant populations. It also applies, perhaps, to studies of culture contact and "integrational development," where the encounter between the folk and the modern is at the heart of large-scale sociohistorical change.

This life history project should therefore be reviewed not in terms of data about interaction gleaned from the narratives themselves but in terms of the dynamics of interactions that comprise the interviews. This discussion reflects my analysis of the taped interviews plus observations recorded in my research journal during the interviews. It would be very beneficial, in pursuing this line of inquiry, to preserve the entire interviews on videotape so that the components of interaction could be assessed by an outside observer, as well as by the interviewer. This process has been advocated and described by Goode (1983:242–46).

For purposes of discussion, as a framework the "main tendency propositions" of Turner that were discussed in chapter 2 will be utilized. The six summary headings will serve our purpose of illustration here, although use of the full propositional inventory might be useful in a more detailed analysis.

1. *Emergence and character of roles.*—It has become clear, the longer I work with retarded people, that they share a fundamental human tendency with persons of normal intelligence, even if they are not able to articulate their expectations. Even though their lives have been quite chaotic (disrupted families, distressing encounters with the juvenile justice and social service systems, a blur of foster homes and quasi-institutional placements), like everyone else, they seek "consistency of behavior" by interpreting all behavior in terms of recognized roles. It is therefore not surprising that they should view me as an au-

thority figure, identified with "staff." Because of the conversational manner adopted during the interviews, I probably seemed most like the staff psychologist to them, an identification that almost certainly predisposed them to talk about themselves to me. (I would like to think that their willingness had something to do with the subtle power of my research technique, but the overall interaction process of role congruence has certainly been the far more important factor.)

It is worth noting that my own process at this point was apt to cause some confusion because my consciously humanitarian outlook would not let me treat these people as clients in the professionally impersonal way that a staff member might. On reflection about the process, however, I have become aware that in treating them as "informants" I conveyed a certain sense of professional detachment in spite of myself. That detachment was naturally interpreted as staff-like by those I interviewed, and, at least in the beginning, it provided a foundation for interaction. We may have been working with different categories of role consistency, but at least we were both engaged in the same process, and our tentative resolutions, though different, were not incompatible.

I was at first puzzled by a narrative gambit employed by my first informants. One man, for example, who had recently run away from his group home and was consequently on some restrictions at the workshop, was telling me about a time some years before when he quarreled with his parole officer, who was telling him to avoid the company of certain old friends: "I got real mad at him. Yeah. I did. Wanted to hit him in his stupid face. I shoulda done the pillow. Yeah. But instead I just yelled at him like a dummy." Another informant, remembering his childhood, when his mother disappeared and his aunt lied and told him she had died, said, "I knew she didn't have no heart attack. Don't ask me how—I just know it. I knew the bitch was lying to me. I shoulda done the pillow, you know, but I couldn't think straight. Hey—I was just a kid. I was throwin' stuff —dirt—all over the old bitch, anything I could find."

This lament about the pillow came up many times. It finally

occurred to me that, in behavior-modification techniques, strong emotions like anger are not suppressed; rather, unacceptable means of expression are replaced by less destructive ones. The clients at OH are frequently counseled by the psychologist to go to their rooms and hit the pillow when they are angry instead of getting into a face-to-face confrontation with other people. The informants, reading me as another psychologist who would probably offer the same advice, anticipated my disapproval of the "inappropriate" demonstrations of anger and presented themselves as having known better (even before they came to OH, where they learned this trick for avoiding trouble) but being simply overcome by extra-strong feelings in times of extreme stress. Their recollections were thus factually untrue—they hadn't known better. What's more, they almost certainly knew that they hadn't felt that way. But, perceiving me as they did, their ability to add that phrase in its proper context in their stories said a great deal—and was eminently truthful to their sense of selfhood as persons working in a particular therapeutic system. It was evidence of a shrewd ability to sort out behavioral cues and build them into an acceptable interactive process.

2. *Role as interaction framework.*—Because role congruence ultimately depends on the dyadic complementarity of roles, the disparity between my initial perception of these informants and their's of me as a psychologist should have led to many a wrong turn. Indeed, if retarded people truly "can never learn," then we would have been stuck at the level of our initial misconceptions, which I, the supposedly intelligent partner, would be the first to recognize.

In fact, it was the informants (at least some of them) who first felt the strain and tried to do something about it. They did so by subtle testing of the waters. "I didn't dry the dishes before I put them away after breakfast," one informant announced to me, apparently apropos of nothing at the start of one session. "I snitched [a staff member's] magazine—you know the one [*Playboy*]," said another a week later. "Hey, I can grow a mustache if I want to—[deleted] what the [deleted] [staff member] says," declared a third. All three of these actions are "bustable" offenses of varying seriousness. The first informant, having failed to get a rise out of me with his confession (more because I wasn't really paying attention to a detail that didn't really fit into the story he was telling than because I didn't know it was something he wasn't supposed to do), began to get an inkling that I wasn't a staff member and apparently said so to his friends, who then tried out their own confessions on me. I didn't react to the second ploy because, again, it was thrown in out of context and I ignored it—another example of that inability to structure a logical narrative sequence discussed in the literature. By the time of the third such incident, I had begun to catch on, and agreed that yes, he did have the right to grow a moustache. (This response was, in fact, true to the program's guidelines; this client had been reprimanded in the past not for wanting to grow a legitimate mustache but because he was lax about regular shaving habits.)

My nonstaff-like reaction, and the fact that I didn't report these delicts, served to convince at least some of the informants that I couldn't be lumped in with the psychologist after all. Where, then, did I fit? I couldn't be an ordinary friend because I didn't live at the group home, but I could be a friendly confidant, a role that certainly fit in reciprocally with my own perceptions. I did, however, need to be careful to avoid becoming a benefactor to the more dependent of the informants inasmuch as that kind of relationship could easily undermine the training program.

3. *Role in relation to actor.*—People tend to continue to play roles that have served them well in the past, at least until they determine that something new is required. Thus, many of my informants "played the dummy" in initial encounters since that was what they were conditioned to play all their lives. It must be remembered, however, that there is no single model of retarded behavior; in fact, the sweet, helpless, childlike, inspirational retarded person stereotype beloved by makers of TV movies was not at all common among the OH informants. Not only were they relatively high functioning (a number of them had lived by their wits on the streets before running afoul of the law), but

most of them adopt a swaggering, can-do pose.

Their most common way of "acting like a retard" is to overdo emotional reactions (throwing violent tantrums if the ring on a soda can snaps or banging their heads on a desk if they have trouble with an arithmetic problem) or to express inappropriate reactions (laughing wildly at a radio news report of a car wreck). A much more subtle variant of the latter is the tendency to deny emotions entirely, and this is the response that I found most commonly in the interviews.

It is certainly true that any number of nonretarded persons also suffer from repressed emotions, but they presumably have the capacity to cover up the problem in a socially appropriate way. My informants, on the other hand, were apt to say things like "And then my mother died—but I didn't care. It didn't mean nothing to me" when it was clear in the context of the larger story that the individual cared very deeply about her. ("Normal" persons, by contrast, would probably express some conventional piety if they felt too ashamed to admit the full extent of their grief—and probably would do the same even if they didn't like their mother.) These informants were less bothered about doing "stupid" things, probably because they are sufficiently functional to learn basic academic and social skills, than about expressing "stupid" feelings. It was their confusion about how to resolve that tension that most clearly marked them as playing out the retarded role that had been assigned to them. Characteristically, it has been their emotions that have gotten them into trouble. They were again saying things that were factually so but emotionally untrue and that made sense only in terms of the role-playing drama of the interview interaction itself. The case of the man who had been raped in jail demonstrates how a non-"staff" response to a display of "inappropriate" emotion evoked a shift in perceived reality. The informant ultimately realized that his emotional response to such a bad experience was appropriate after all and that there were ways to distinguish the experiences that legitimately elicit strong emotional response from those that do not.

4. *Role in organizational settings.*—Because the interviews

were conducted on the premises of OH and with its consent, they were inevitably seen by the informants as agency functions. Even if I could not be thought of as a staff member, the interviews could be built into a behavior-modification schedule, and so a natural limit was placed on the ability of our interactions to grow. However, a fact of life for retarded persons that must always be kept in mind is that they function within a system whose objective rules are made by others and that their personalities, as well as their cultural awareness, are bound by the kinds of interaction that are permitted by organizational conventions.

5. *Role in social settings.*—Having adopted the protective coloration of the "dummy" role, many informants tended to allow other roles to slip into that larger rubric. For example, despite their intellectual deficiencies, a number of them are really quite adept at other pursuits. But they tend to keep these other skills under wraps because they have learned that people think of them as "retards" and will automatically devalue anything they do, even if they do it well. (The obverse is also sometimes true: "normal" people sometimes patronize retarded people by overpraising their accomplishments when they accomplish the simplest little thing, or do something the retarded persons themselves know has been done inadequately. One of the clients, a fairly talented runner, adamantly refused to participate in Special Olympics. I asked him why. "I don't want no old white lady hugging on me just for crossing the finish line," he shrugged.) One informant has a nice voice, a love of country music, and an astonishing ability to mimic the records he hears on the radio. He demonstrated his talent in the course of one interview. Since we had earlier been talking about his largely unsuccessful efforts to impress a certain (nonretarded) young woman he had met at the laundromat, I suggested that he sing for her because I was sure she'd enjoy his voice. "No," he said sadly but firmly. "Nobody wants to listen to no dummy singing."

6. *Role and the person.*—The self-conceptions of my informants are largely colored by the image of "the retarded" imposed by the mainstream. Yet they are placed in "training" situations in

which they are bombarded with the message that they must learn to be like "everyone else" in order to get by in society. Their lives are thus built up of critical encounters in which they try to be "like everyone else" while an inner voice is reminding them that they are bound to fail because, after all, they are "just dummies." Even when they do succeed, that inner voice gets in the way, telling them not to trust that success. The tension is usually resolved by a negative retreat to the ugly, but at least familiar, stereotype.

One informant, for example, told me at length about a horse farm where he had lived happily for a brief time as a boy. It was perhaps the most complex and sustained single narrative I recorded from the OH men, and it was told with warm and fully "appropriate" emotion, using surprisingly sophisticated, metaphorical imagery (a favorite horse was "a black windstorm"). It was a remarkable performance, and I told him immediately how much I'd enjoyed hearing him tell about the farm. Much to my surprise, he suddenly jumped up, swept my coffee mug off the table, and stormed out of the room with a curse. After he'd calmed down, he said, "Don't be mad. What can you expect from a dummy?" Later still he told me, talking about another subject entirely, that he could never stand praise because only "phonies" ever said nice things to him. I realized that, in telling me his horse story, he was opening up his most cherished, private, secure inner world. My response, which I meant sincerely, rang the wrong bell for him since it sounded like the words of all the patronizing phonies he had ever encountered. Because I had inadvertently treated him like a "retard," he responded by revoking my privileged pass into his inner world, by acting in a stereotypically "retarded" manner.

Did he ever actually live on that farm, or did he merely see it in a movie, or hear someone else talk about it? If I were collecting a documented case history, that question would have been meaningful. But, as it was, the symbolic importance of that farm to his sense of self far transcended its literal, historical truth. And his ability to use that reminiscence, factual or otherwise, to include me in his world was evidence of the evolution of

his consciousness. Alas, my response served only to convince
him that he had gone too far, risked too much. He still needed
the security of resolving the tension among the different parts of
his self, even if that meant settling for the most negative aspect
of his self-image.

The experience of this informant may be compared with that
of a retarded informant discussed by Turner (1980). This man
learned, midway through the collection of his life story, that he
had been misdiagnosed in childhood; he was not retarded after
all as far as his IQ was concerned (although, after years in
institutional and training settings, his behavioral repertoire made
him seem as if he were). His self-image seemed to change
overnight. He no longer identified himself as "retarded," and he
professed to be out of sympathy with all those who had been his
companions and friends just hours before. Moreover, he insisted
on retelling many of the incidents of his life that had already
been recorded, this time reinterpreted from the point of view of
one who was wrongfully stigmatized, rather than as one who
accepted his status as retarded.

In summary, I have come to the conclusion that, at least when
working with informants who are in a situation of forced
encounter with a more or less inimical "mainstream" culture, the
process of creating a life history reveals as much about the
culture of the informant as does the narrative text—if a usable
text is even created. The concepts of symbolic interactionist
analysis can be used to give some definition to the study of this
phenomenon and to cast it in terms that may make one "particu-
laristic" encounter comparable to others, much as the literary
critic of autobiography seeks comparability not in the details of
subjects' lives, but in the narrative techniques used to construct
those evanescent "metaphors of self."

7 /
Social Meaning and Symbolic
Interaction

THE ENDURING POPULARITY of autobiographical materials in social research rests on the capacity of the life history method to elicit specific data of an intensely personal nature that sheds light on the details of large-scale social and historical events, as well as of the individual personality. They are both ethnographic and psychological documents of wide-ranging application. Taken singly, they can function as case histories, by which representative people come to typify the dynamics of personality development in a particular sociocultural setting. When the setting is a past period of history, and the individual subject is an "extraordinary" person who has left his or her mark on the times, the psychohistorical approach enables us to understand how the leader, by embodying the tensions of a particular era, seizes the historical moment and provides vicarious resolution for the many. Taken in the collective, the personal narratives of people related in time and by circumstances can provide an impressionistic mosaic of a society.

But if the lead of the literary critics is followed, this results in a realization of the limits of the autobiographical text, which is less a factual re-creation of life than a deliberately shaped "metaphor" of the self—a work of art, in other words. This perception leads to a suggestion of yet another possible role for the life history method—a role in which the act of interviewing, the process of active re-creation of that metaphor of self, comes to be as much a matter of emphasis and analysis as is the "factual" text itself.

The working definition of "self" in such cases must be essentially transcultural: whatever it is in terms of particular behaviors, it arises out of and takes its meaning from critical, "dramatic" social interactions. The nature of that drama will, of course, depend on a given culture's expectations about narrative form. The life history elicitation interview thus becomes a provisional microcosm of the interaction process that is typical of a culture, such that it matters less what the informant says about his or her "self" than it does how the self emerges from the structuring of the interaction. The interviewer and subject conspire to construct a version of the self—and the strategies they employ in that conspiracy will probably derive from the shared, unspoken regularities of interaction expectations in their culture.

That even retarded people can recognize and manipulate those rules is an indication of how deeply ingrained they are. Even if the informant and the interviewer come from different cultures, the ways in which they shift to meet on common ground explain how culture can be manipulated—not only to enhance "adaptation to the environment" but also to provide a satisfactory definition of one's identity with regard to significant others.

The image of self created by the particular interaction may be evanescent, but I propose that the process—the strategies used to create those shifting images—will be relatively constant, reflecting not only the informant's personality makeup and particular socialization experiences but also the larger sociocultural forces that shaped the particular experiences.

In the last analysis, the life history text blends the consciousness of the informant and the interviewer, so that the text becomes a "shadow biography" of the researcher, not simply an objective life story "as told to" (Frank 1978:24; see also Bogdan and Taylor 1975). In that sense, even if the life history data are not used in a psychotherapeutic sense, the process itself may be therapeutic in the sense that any creative effort can provide this benefit. As Whittemore, Koegel, and Langness (1980:25) note: "After all of our scientific justification for the proliferation of these histories, we feel there is a compelling argument for the life story affording some retarded individuals a monumental opportunity to entertain, engage in, and identify with the process of making their own worthwhile contribution." This observation can apply equally well to other "disadvantaged" people, and it is certainly not inapplicable to "normal" informants.

In summarizing these reflections, it can be said that the life history is a document of selfhood that emerges from particular kinds of interactive encounters. The self that is elicited is not a timeless, finished product but is rather a fragment of an evolving process. In essence, then, the life history text need not be factual in order to be true.

Indeed, in reviewing the materials I have collected to date from my retarded informants for example, I am struck by the amount of information that I know is in error; I can only speculate as to how much of the rest of the material is also technically "wrong." Such doubts would invalidate the collection if the research interest was solely in the texts as objective sources of data, whether psychological or social.

The incorrectness of these documents could certainly be cited as a reason for ignoring retarded people as capable informants about the circumstances of their own lives, and for interviewing them mostly as case studies in individual pathology. I propose, however, that retarded people are, indeed, bearers of culture insofar as they have internalized interactive strategies of one sort or another. That some of these strategies may be psychotherapeutically unwholesome is less significant in this context than the fact that they are logical and coherent approaches to defining a person's identity and allowing it to develop in the course of a meaningful social interaction.

But one must surely ask: Why are these life histories "wrong"? My view is that it is not a lack of intelligence that causes the informants to speak falsely; most of them are capable of learning all sorts of fact-based skills and incorporating them into their daily lives. Even those in the group who are psychiatrically disordered are not clinically delusional. I can only surmise that there is a deliberate attempt to create fiction. Certainly they may have done so out of a desire to thwart the representative of an authority system that has never been anything but unfeeling toward them. But, in my judgment, as the process went on, that motive receded. It might also be suggested, in Freudian terms, that people wounded by unhappy life experiences would prefer to tell lies rather than rehash the ugly reality. However, my most creative liars tend to be not the ones who seek to brighten the bad times but the ones who make their lives seem even more Dickensian in their horror and squalor than they really have been.

I conclude, therefore, that the "self" emerges most readily among retarded people—as among all people denied the right of ordinary social interaction with those of higher status or greater power—when they are given the opportunity to work on a collaborative effort of creation. But to do so is threatening because it is so unfamiliar, and the rights so casually proffered could so easily be withdrawn by the critical "audience." So it is easier to create behind a protective screen of symbol and metaphor. But, after all, pleasure can be had in making up and sharing such fantasy, even among nonretarded people. The overt content of many myths or even children's fairy tales is quite horrible, and yet their telling is pleasurable, and the act of sharing them is one of the most potent of all social bonds. And, as anthropologists have long known, more psychological and cultural truth can sometimes be found in such fantasies, which are passed down through time, than can be found in passing "reality."

It is said that when Henry Schoolcraft tried to learn about the lives of the Indians he was sent to administer in the early nineteenth century, he was startled to realize that the "savages" told stories. The prevailing opinion was that primitive people had no interior life capable of generating and sharing mythology. Retarded people have suffered from the same stigmatization, but in fact they can create myths and draw the nonretarded interviewer into the process of creation. The result is not off-the-wall irrelevancy but stories with structure and direction. The retarded can take pride and pleasure in working with other people in that creative act, and its study holds much promise for life history research not only with these retarded informants but for the study of identity and cultural process in general.

References Cited

Allport, Gordon. 1945. "The use of personal documents in psychological science." In *The Use of Personal Documents in History, Anthropology, and Sociology,* edited by L. Gottschalk, C. Kluckhohn, and R. Angell. New York: Social Science Research Council Bulletin no. 53.

Angell, R. 1945. "A critical review of the development of the personal document method in sociology, 1920–1940." In *The Uses of Personal Documents in History, Anthropology, and Sociology,* edited by L. Gottschalk, C. Kluckhohn, and R. Angell. New York: Social Science Research Council Bulletin no. 53.

Angrosino, Michael V. 1974. *Outside Is Death: Community Organization, Ideology, and Alcoholism among the East Indians of Trinidad.* Winston-Salem, NC: Overseas Research Center.

————. 1976. "The use of autobiography as 'life history': the case of Albert Gomes." *Ethos* 4:133–54.

————. 1981. *Quality Assurance for Community Care of Retarded Adults in Tennessee.* Nashville: Vanderbilt University Institute for Public Policy Studies.

————. 1982. "Personal narratives and cultural complexity: an oral anthropology of Aruba, Netherlands Antilles." *Oral History Review* 10:93–118.

————. 1985. "Sexuality education for mentally retarded adults: theory and practice." Paper read at American Anthropological Association (Washington DC).

————. 1986. "Son and lover: the anthropologist as nonthreatening male." In *Self, Sex, and Gender in Cross-Cultural Fieldwork,* edited by T. Whitehead and M. E. Conaway. Urbana: University of Illinois Press.

Angrosino, Michael V., and Linda M. Whiteford. 1986. "Service delivery, advocacy, and the policy cycle." In *Current Health Policy Issues and Alternatives: An Applied Social Science Perspective,* edited by Carole E. Hill. Atlanta: University of Georgia Press.

Aries, Philippe. 1965. *Centuries of Childhood.* Translated by R. Baldick. New York: Vintage.

Babad, Elisha Y., Max Birnbaum, and Kenneth D. Benne. 1983. *The Social Self: Group Influences on Personal Identity.* Beverly Hills, CA: Sage.

Balan, J., H. L. Browning, and E. Jelin. 1973. *Men in a Developing Society: Geographic and Social Mobility in Monterey, Mexico.* Austin: University of Texas Press.

Barnouw, Victor. 1985. *Culture and Personality,* 4th ed. Homewood, IL: Dorsey.

Bercovici, Sylvia. 1981. "Qualitative methods and cultural perspectives in the study of deinstitutionalization." In *Deinstitutionalization and Community Adjustment of Mentally Retarded People,* edited by R. H. Bruininks et al. Washington: American Association on Mental Deficiency.

Bertaux, Daniel. 1981a. "From the life history approach to the transformation of sociological practice." In *Biography and Society: The Life History Approach in the Social Sciences,* edited by Daniel Bertaux. Beverly Hills, CA: Sage.

————. 1981b. "Introduction." In *Biography and Society: The Life History Approach in the Social Sciences,* edited by Daniel Bertaux, Beverly Hills, CA: Sage.

Blasing, M. K. 1977. *The Art of Life: Studies in American Autobiographical Literature.* Austin: University of Texas Press.

Blassingame, John W. 1973. "Black autobiographies as histories and literature." *Black Scholar* 5:2–9.

Blythe, Ronald. 1974. *Akenfield: Portrait of an English Village.* New York: Vintage.

Bock, Philip K. 1980. *Continuities in Psychological Anthropology.* San Francisco: Freeman.

Bogdan, R., and S. J. Taylor. 1975. "The judged, not the judges: an insider's view of mental retardation." *American Psychologist* 31:47–52.

Bruss, Elizabeth W. 1976. *Autobiographical Acts: The Changing Situation of a Literary Genre.* Baltimore: Johns Hopkins University Press.

Catani, Maurizio. 1973. *Journal de Mohamed.* Paris: Stock 2, Collection Temoignier.

————. 1975. "Les histoires de vie sociale, instrument critique des pratiques et objets sociologiques." In *Compte Rendus de Recherches et Bibliographiques Sur L'Immigration.* Paris: ERSMOI, Centre d'Etudes Sociologiques.

————. 1981. "Social-life history as ritualized oral exchange." In *Biography and Society: The Life History Approach in the Social Sciences,* edited by Daniel Bertaux. Beverly Hills, CA: Sage.

Cicourel, Aaron V. 1973. *Cognitive Sociology.* London: Macmillan.

Crane, Julia G. 1987. *Saba Silhouettes.* New York: Vantage.

Crapanzano, Vincent. 1980. *Tuhami: Portrait of a Moroccan.* Chicago: University of Chicago Press.

_____. 1984 "Life histories." *American Anthropologist* 86:953–60.

De Mause, Lloyd. 1975. *The History of Childhood.* New York: Harper.

Denzin, Norman K. 1981. "The interactionist study of social organization: a note on method." In *Biography and Society: The Life History Approach in the Social Sciences,* edited by Daniel Bertaux. Beverly Hills, CA: Sage.

Dollard, John. 1935. *Criteria for the Life History.* New Haven: Yale University Press.

Du Bois, Cora. 1944. *The People of Alor.* Minneapolis: University of Minnesota Press.

Eakin, Paul John. 1985. *Fictions in Autobiography: Studies in the Art of Self-Invention.* Princeton: Princeton University Press.

Earle, William. 1972. *The Autobiographical Consciousness: A Philosophical Inquiry into Existence.* Chicago: Quadrangle.

Edgerton, Robert B. 1967. *The Cloak of Competence: Stigma in the Lives of the Mentally Retarded.* Berkeley: University of California Press.

_____. 1970. "Mental retardation in non-western societies: toward a cross-cultural perspective on incompetence." In *Social-Cultural Aspects of Mental Retardation,* edited by H. Carl Haywood. New York: Appleton-Century-Crofts.

_____. 1979. *Mental Retardation.* Cambridge, MA: Harvard University Press.

_____. 1984 "Introduction." In *Lives in Process: Mildly Retarded Adults in a Large City,* edited by Robert Edgerton. Washington: American Association on Mental Deficiency.

Elder, Glen. 1981. "History and the life course." In *Biography and Society: The Life History Approach in the Social Sciences,* edited by Daniel Bertaux. Beverly Hills, CA: Sage.

Erikson, Erik H. 1958. *Young Man Luther.* New York: Norton.

_____. 1963. *Childhood and Society.* 2d ed. New York: Norton.

_____. 1968. *Identity, Youth and Crisis.* New York: Norton

_____. 1969. *Gandhi's Truth.* New York: Norton.

_____. 1975. *Life History and the Historical Movement.* New York: Norton.

Evans, Daryl Paul. 1983. *The Lives of Mentally Retarded People.* Boulder, CO: Westview.

Fenna, D., et al. 1976. "Ethanol metabolism in various racial groups." In *Cross-Cultural Approaches to the Study of Alcohol,* edited by M. W. Everett, J. O. Waddell, and D. B. Heath. The Hague: Mouton.

Ferrarotti, Franco. 1981. "On the autonomy of the biographical method." Translated by Anne Draatz. In *Biography and Society: The Life History Approach in the Social Sciences,* edited by Daniel Bertaux. Beverly Hills, CA: Sage.

Frank, Gelya. 1978. "Finding the common denominator: a phenomenological critique of life history method." Working Paper #2, Sociobehavioral Group, Mental Retardation Research Center, School of Medicine, UCLA.

Freed, Ruth S. and Stanley A. Freed. 1985. *The Psychomedical Case History of a Low-Caste Woman of North India.* New York: American Museum of Natural History.

Gladwin, Thomas, and Seymour B. Sarason. 1953. *Truk: Man in Paradise.* New York: Viking Fund Publications in Anthropology #20.

Goffman, Erving. 1967. *Interaction Ritual.* Garden City, NY: Doubleday Anchor.

Gomes, Albert. 1974. *Through a Maze of Colour.* Port of Spain: Key Caribbean Publications.

Goode, David A. 1983. "Who is Bobby? ideology and method in the discovery of a Down's Syndrome person's competence." In *Health Through Occupation: Theory and Practice in Occupational Therapy,* edited by Gary Kielhofer. Philadelphia: F. A. Davis.

Green, Vera. 1976. "Voluntary associations: a key to the study of complex societies." Manuscript.

Hankiss, Agnes. 1981. "Ontologies of the self: on the mythological rearranging of one's life history." In *Biography and Society: The Life History Approach in the Social Sciences,* edited by Daniel Bertaux. Beverly Hills, CA: Sage.

Haywood, H. Carl. 1970. "Some perspectives on socio-cultural aspects of mental retardation." In *Social-Cultural Aspects of Mental Retardation,* edited by H. Carl Haywood. New York: Appleton-Century-Crofts.

Henry, Jules. 1945. "Review of *People of Alor*." *American Journal of Orthopsychiatry* 15:372–73.

Hunt, Nigel. 1967. *The World of Nigel Hunt: The Diary of a Mongoloid Youth.* Beaconsfield: Darwen Finlayson Ltd.

Jellinek, E. M. 1960. *The Disease Concept of Alcoholism.* New Haven: College and University Press.

Kernan, Keith T., and Sharon Sabsay. 1985. "Referential first mention in narratives by mildly retarded adults." Working Paper #30. Sociobehavioral Group, Mental Retardation Research Center, School of Medicine, UCLA.

Kluckhohn, Clyde. 1945. "The personal document in anthropological science." In *The Use of Personal Documents in History, Anthropology, and Sociology,* edited by L. Gottschalk, C. Kluckhohn, and R. Angell. New York: Social Science Research Council Bulletin no. 53.

Kohli, Martin. 1981. "Biography: account, text, method." In *Biography and Society: The Life History Approach in the Social Sciences,* edited by Daniel Bertaux. Beverly Hills, CA: Sage.

Langness, L.L. 1965. *The Life History in Anthropological Science.* New York: Holt, Rinehart and Winston.

Langness, L.L., and Gelya Frank. 1981. *Lives: An Anthropological Approach to Biography.* Novato, CA: Chandler and Sharp.

Langness, L.L., and Harold G. Levine. 1986. *Culture and Retardation.* Dordrecht: D. Reidel.

Leighton, Alexander H. 1959. *My Name Is Legion.* New York: Basic Books.

Lewis, Oscar. 1961. *The Children of Sanchez.* New York: Random House.
_____. 1968. *La Vida.* New York: Random House.

Lewis, Oscar, Ruth M. Lewis, and Susan M. Rigdon. 1977. *Living the Revolution: An Oral History of Contemporary Cuba.* 3 vols. Urbana: University of Illinois Press.

Linder, Steve. 1978. "Language context and the evolution of the verbal competence of the mentally retarded." Working Paper #1, Sociobehavioral Group, Mental Retardation Research Center, School of Medicine, UCLA.

Loewenberg, Peter. 1971. "The psychohistorical origins of the Nazi youth cohort." *American Historical Review* 76:1487–1502.

MacAndrew, Craig, and Robert Edgerton. 1967. *Drunken Comportment.* Chicago: Aldine.

McCune, Billy. 1973. *The Autobiography of Billy McCune.* San Francisco: Straight Arrow Books.

Mandel, Barrett J. 1980. "Full of life now." In *Autobiography: Essays Theoretical and Critical,* edited by James Olney. Princeton: Princeton University Press.

Mandelbaum, David G. 1973. "The study of life history: Gandhi." *Current Anthropology* 14:177–206.

Mazlish, Bruce. 1975. *James and John Stuart Mill: Father and Son in the Nineteenth Century.* New York: Basic Books.

Mehlman, Jeffrey. 1974. *A Structural Study of Autobiography: Proust, Leiris, Sartre, Lévi-Strauss.* Ithaca: Cornell University Press.

Olney, James. 1972. *Metaphors of Self: The Meaning of Autobiography.* Princeton: Princeton University Press.

―――――. 1980. "Autobiography and the cultural moment: a thematic, historical, and bibliographical introduction." In *Autobiography: Essays Theoretical and Critical,* edited by James Olney. Princeton: Princeton University Press.

Parsons, Talcott. 1972. "Definitions of health and illness in the light of American values and social structure." In *Patients, Physicians, and Illness,* edited by E. G. Jaco. New York: Free Press.

Pattison, E. Mansell, Mark B. Sobell, and Linda C. Sobell. 1977. *Emerging Concepts of Alcohol Dependence.* New York: Springer.

Peacock, James L., and A. Thomas Kirsch. 1970. *The Human Direction: An Evolutionary Approach to Social and Cultural Anthropology.* New York: Appleton-Century-Crofts.

Prisco, Salvatore. 1980. *An Introduction to Psychohistory: Theories and Case Studies.* Lanham, MD: University Press of America.

Renza, Louis A. 1980. "The veto of the imagination: a theory of autobiography." In *Autobiography: Essays Theoretical and Critical,* edited by James Olney. Princeton: Princeton University Press.

Sartre, Jean-Paul. 1964. *Saint Genet: Actor and Martyr.* Translated by Bernard Fruchtman. New York: George Braziller.

Schutz, A., and T. Luckmann. 1974. *The Structure of the Life-World.* London: Heineman.

Seagoe, May V. 1964. *Yesterday Was Tuesday, All Day and All Night: The Story of a Unique Education.* Boston: Little-Brown.

Shaw, Clifford. 1930. *The Jack-Roller: A Delinquent Boy's Own Story.* Chicago: University of Chicago Press.

Sigelman, Carol K., et al. 1981. "Issues in interviewing mentally retarded persons: an empirical study." In *Deinstitutionalization and Community Adjustment of Mentally Retarded People,* edited by R. H. Bruininks et al. Washington: American Association on Mental Deficiency.

Simmons, Leo, ed. 1942. *Sun Chief: The Autobiography of a Hopi Indian.* New Haven: Yale University Press.

Spengemann, William C. 1980. *The Forms of Autobiography: Episodes in the History of a Literary Genre.* New Haven: Yale University Press.

Spiro, Melford E. 1972. "An overview and suggested reorientation." In *Psychological Anthropology,* edited by F.L.K. Hsu. Cambridge MA: Schenkman.

Starobinski, Jean. 1980. "The style of autobiography." Translated by Seymour Chatman. In *Autobiography: Essays Theoretical and Critical,* edited by James Olney. Princeton: Princeton University Press.

Straus, Robert. 1974. *Escape from Custody.* New York: Harper and Row.

Szcepanski, Jan. 1981. "The use of autobiographies in historical social psychology." In *Biography and Society: The Life History Approach in the Social Sciences,* edited by Daniel Bertaux. Beverly Hills, CA: Sage.

Thomas, William I., and Florian Znaniecki. 1958. *The Polish Peasant in Europe and America.* 2 vols. New York: Dover. (Originally published 1917–18.)

Turner, Jim L. 1980. "Yes, I am human: autobiography of a 'retarded career.'" *Journal of Community Psychology* 8:3–8.

Turner, Ralph H. 1968. "Social roles: sociological aspects." In *International Encyclopedia of the Social Sciences.* New York: Macmillan.

Weber, Max. 1964. *Basic Concepts in Sociology.* New York: Citadel Press.

White, Robert W. 1952. *Lives in Progress.* New York: Holt, Rinehart and Winston.

Whittemore, Robert D., Paul Koegel, and L.L. Langness. 1980. "The life history approach to mental retardation." Working Paper #12, Sociobehavioral Group, Mental Retardation Research Center, School of Medicine, UCLA.

Wilson, Peter J. 1973. *Crab Antics: The Social Anthropology of English-Speaking Negro Societies in the Caribbean.* New Haven: Yale University Press.

————. 1974. *Oscar: An Inquiry into the Nature of Sanity.* New York: Vintage.

Wyngaarden, Marty. 1981. "Interviewing mentally retarded persons: issues and strategies." In *Deinstitutionalization and Community Adjustment of Mentally Retarded People,* edited by R.H. Bruininks et al. Washington: American Association on Mental Deficiency.

Zetlin, Andrea S., and Jim Turner. 1984. "Self-perspectives on being handicapped: stigma and adjustment." In *Lives in Process: Mildly Retarded Adults in a Large City,* edited by Robert Edgerton. Washington: American Association on Mental Deficiency.

Index

A.A. *See* Alcoholics Anonymous

Afro-American Studies: and autobiography, 6

Aging: studies of, 16

Akenfield, 64–65

Alcoholics Anonymous: and alcoholic recovery, 30

Alcoholism: in cross-cultural perspective, 32–33; as a culture-bound phenomenon, 32–33; and current medical opinion, 32; and the transcultural psychiatric theory, 29

Alor, 18

American Studies: and autobiography, 6

Angelou, Maya, 6

Antithetical strategy: and autobiography, 11. *See also* Autobiography

Aruba: and increased rate of change, 67–68; Lago, 78; migrants, 68–69; and single women, 76–78; and social differentiation, 69–72; Social Work Department, 77; and Surinamers, 71; and universalization, 73–76. *See also* Caribbean

Autobiography: American approach to, 13; as an artifact, 10; definition of, 3, 5, 10; European approach to, 13–14; and historical social psychology, 42; strategies of, 10–11

Biography: definition of, 3

Boas, Franz: attitude toward life history, 13

Boswell, James, 7

Caribbean: and Aruba, 66–69; founding of Lago, 68–71; and the island of Saba, 63–64; and political-economic life, 63

Chalasiński, Josef, 14

Chicago School, 14

Cleaver, Eldridge, 12

Community-based treatment agencies: in Florida, 80

Compensatory strategy: and autobiography, 11. *See also* Autobiography

Crapanzano, Vincent: and dynamic models, 21; and *Tuhami: Portrait of a Moroccan,* 19

Culture shock: experienced by fieldworkers, 23

Current literary theory: view on autobiography, 3–4

Deinstitutionalization policy, 80

Douglass, Frederick, 6

Dynastic strategy: and autobiography, 10. *See also* Autobiography

Edgerton, Robert: and *The Cloak of Competence,* 81–82

Equiano, Olaudah, 6

Erikson, Eric: and psychohistorical approach, 44–47. *See also* Psychohistory

Franklin, Ben, 11

Gandhi, 44

115